MODERN ENGLISH SCULPTURE

Modern English Sculpture

A. M. HAMMACHER

41 COLOUR PLATES
87 BLACK AND WHITE ILLUSTRATIONS

THAMES AND HUDSON · LONDON

There are two dates that are decisively important to the English in regard to their conviction that an English sculpture of international significance not only existed (of which the insiders were fully aware), but was also accepted. These were the year 1948, when Henry Moore was awarded the International Prize for Sculpture at the Venice Biennale Exhibition, and the year 1952, when at the Biennale, the British Pavilion showed works by eight young English sculptors (among them Butler, Chadwick, Armitage and Paolozzi). In the case of Moore, it could have been suggested that he had an exceptionally personal talent, not to be explained by any English tradition. When however it proved to be possible to make a choice of younger artists whose style was different from, and even opposed to Moore's principles, all indecision was vanquished. As Herbert Read expressed it in *The Ambiguous Critic,* '. . . even Paris had to admit the existence of an English sculptor.'

But acceptance on the Continent of an English sculpture was only an external factor. It had already existed earlier without the continental aesthetico-social distinction, and even before the second World War it had gained a victory, not acknowledged everywhere, but incontestably real, over a vacillating past and a domineering *Ecole de Paris.*

Throughout her history, England had failed to come forward with sculpture of importance. There had been anonymous Anglo-Norman carving; a vigorous sculpture in stone and wood in and outside the cathedrals and a charming production of panels and images in alabaster which became an industry and lasted into the fifteenth century. But this was the work of English craftsmen who, with insular seclusion from the continent, practised the applied arts, in particular for the production of decorations, furniture and goldsmith's work.

Up till the present no English critic or historian has written a more or less complete survey of the amazing phenomenon that in this country in the twentieth century, within less than fifty years, a sculpture came into being which not only held its own beside continental European sculpture, but which even determined to an important extent the aspect of twentieth-century sculpture.

It is true that excellent essays, introductions to catalogues and monographs have been written: Herbert Read, J.P. Hodin and David Sylvester have published eminently clever works. Alan Bowness and Robert Melville continue their activities as art critics successfully. Questions: Was there a hesitation that had to be surmounted? Did the hypercritical English acumen prevent people from seeing the national production in an international context? It is undoubtedly true that the English history of sculpture, in the important context of a characteristically local artistic life, is still awaiting its English exposition.

Here follows, as seen from the continent, a first sketch, written from experience of the slow and not always clear image of the plastic figure of the Anglo-Saxons, whom formerly we were inclined to consider almost non-existent as plastic artists. A country that does not become conscious of three dimensions (in architecture and sculpture), and does not manifest itself accordingly lacks something essential. It may be important in literature, in dramatic art, in music, but if the palpably visual world remains untouched, the social and personally creative image of this particular community lacks an essential dimension.

Did Anglo-Saxon sculpture really come into existence out of a vacuum? Nothing is born without a period of preparation, of incubation. It may be that the pre-natal stage was invisible, yet we are forced to suppose it was there. Without doubt it had something to do with the continental development of art in the twentieth century, which can more easily be traced than the inner urges that stimulated the creation of a fertile atmosphere for plastic art in England, and more especially in London.

As the teaching of art is always inferior to the creation of art itself, art

JACOB EPSTEIN - *Third group of Marble Doves, 1914-15*

schools can never guarantee development of eminent creative talents that are latent in a people. But certainly in England, and especially there, the way in which art lessons are given, their extent and their quality, is important to the technical training of incipient artists or sensitive persons who feel attracted to art teaching.

Though it is well known that the attitude taken up by young artists leads them to deny that they ever learned anything of importance in the academies and art schools, it is a striking fact that many of the older and younger sculptors have attended during a certain period the lessons in one or two of the four types of art schools to be found in England. Apart from the Royal College of Art and the Royal Academy of Arts (founded in 1768) there are as many as 175 local art schools, as well as university art schools and private schools. The Royal College, subsidized by the government, was originally intended to train pupils for industry, but became in fact a real school of art, also for the training of art teachers.

The Slade School (founded in 1869) has become an important institution and the art school of Leeds should also be mentioned.

The training for commercial art and of artists and craftsmen for industry was already established in the nineteenth century, the time of the industrial revolution, which received more attention in England than elsewhere. We find in the biographies of most *avant-garde* sculptors of the present the names of the schools appearing repeatedly: Slade, Leeds, Chelsea, St Martins, Bath, Sheffield. Often students, who in the meantime have become well known, return to a school in the function of a regular or part-time teacher, so that generations may benefit from a training which of course is always inclined to become 'academic' in the unfavourable sense of the word, but which renews itself and certainly has laid the foundations, also for the later *avant-garde* artists, of a technical schooling. This must not remain ignored as a social element to be compared with the more artistic and personal element of what the continental and particularly the Paris atmosphere has brought about in teaching.

In 1886, the New English Art Club with the late acceptance of French impressionism insularly fructified a continental tradition. After Whistler, Steer and Sickert especially played an important part and they paved the way for the fertilization of those trends that became important after impressionism (Van Gogh, Gauguin, Cézanne, Seurat). As yet this only related to painting. It is true that Rodin was known in England, but there is not the slightest indication of a visible influence. However, by about 1900 there must have been an awakening sculptural consciousness among the artists. A first proof of this was what Charles Ricketts wrote about Rodin in the letters and diaries that were so important in regard to artistic life in London from towards the end of the nineteenth century until well into the first World War. One would hardly expect Ricketts, with his romantically decorative talent, to harbour plastic aspirations and still less such a critical vision of Rodin's work. To prove to what extent Rodin influenced the artistic perception and the critical sense, also in England, a quotation may follow here.

'27 November 1900:

Rodin remains the one possible surprise among contemporaries, and the only man whose work one cannot anticipate. The sight of his things stirred up curious old wishes of mine to do sculpture. I can imagine a large original field for the sculptor that should take form under totally different technical conditions from those mastered by Rodin, sculpture that would avoid all painters' tendencies to loose handling and study nothing since the traces of Myron, excepting Michelangelo and Barye. A sculpture in full hard relief, with the use of marble and polish and oil; some of the works to be done in wood, mostly in bronze; often without pedestals; sculpture that would arrest the light, not play with it. All art is now landscape art, even Rodin has, in a sense, been influenced by the landscape standard of light and shade and so on.'

When in 1917 Rodin died in a world more than ever full of the din of war, Ricketts wrote what he called himself an 'ungracious and ungrateful' commemorative article on Rodin in which he stated, however, that he had 'an immense influence and stimulus upon my life'. It is clear that there is a reaction to Rodin, 'who had played on the verge of bad taste in sentiment and form, fallen into the Baroque and done work to surprise the critic. His art had grown less and less certain since the Balzac, which was magnificent in its preliminary studies, almost worthless in its result.'

What Ricketts expected, namely 'a large original field for the sculptor that should take form under totally different technical conditions from those mastered by Rodin', and a release from the pictorial and the landscape, did not materialize immediately.

The years after the first World War became of great importance.

A turning away from impressionism occurred, but towards that absorption of the complex world which is called for the sake of convenience 'postimpressionism', and in which the famous art critic Roger Fry played a prominent part. At the same time the artistic climate was determined to a high degree by literature. The so-called Bloomsbury Group was the centre, where the novelist Virginia Woolf and her husband Leonard as well as Roger Fry were the leaders (without any intentions or awareness, as Leonard Woolf declares in his autobiography, to impose themselves as such). Vanessa and Clive Bell joined them, also Lytton Strachey, Duncan Grant, J.M. Keynes, Desmond McCarthy and E.M. Forster. The psychoanalytic doctrines became known. The painters regrouped themselves. Thomas Ernest Hulme (1883-1917) was the young poetic philosopher who was a friend of the poet Ezra Pound during the latter's London period (1908-20). Hulme and Pound were already more advanced in their appreciation than the Bloomsbury Group. London began to develop some attraction for young foreign sculptors, which could not be caused by English sculpture since it hardly existed at all, but was certainly brought about by the atmosphere that had been created.

The Italian futurist Marinetti came to London to give lectures, in 1910 in the Lyceum Club, in 1912 in the Bechstein Hall, and again in the Doré Gallery in 1914. He created commotion and a fierce rejection of futurism in the circles round Hulme and Pound, who became the literary and philosophical defenders of two young sculptors from abroad: Jacob Epstein (1880-1959) who arrived in London in 1905 from New York after a relatively short stay in Paris, and Henri Gaudier-Brzeska (1891-1915), who came to London in December 1910. The rejection of futurism was not reactionary in character; it was based on differently coloured *avant-garde* ideas which, under the name of vorticism, indicated a kind of programme.

Ossip Zadkine, who made sculpture at the age of fifteen when he came from Smolensk to London for the first time in 1905, returned there in 1913 and 1914 to participate in two exhibitions at the invitation of Henri Gaudier-Brzeska. But a bad reception at Epstein's on the occasion of his first stay in London had depressed him, and he eventually showed a preference for Paris.

So in sculpture we find two foreigners, Epstein and Gaudier, who familiarized themselves so intensely with the artistic London atmosphere that the moment of struggle for recognition, individual and social, had arrived. Although this was not immediately achieved, the attempt would have been unthinkable without critics and literary writers such as Hulme and Pound. Hulme was a follower of Bergson. Pound was a poet with a generous cultural turn of mind, who was a bellicose figure in literature, and who did not shrink from repulsing the violent attacks on Epstein and, even many

BARBARA HEPWORTH - *Marble form (Mycenae)*, 1959

8

9

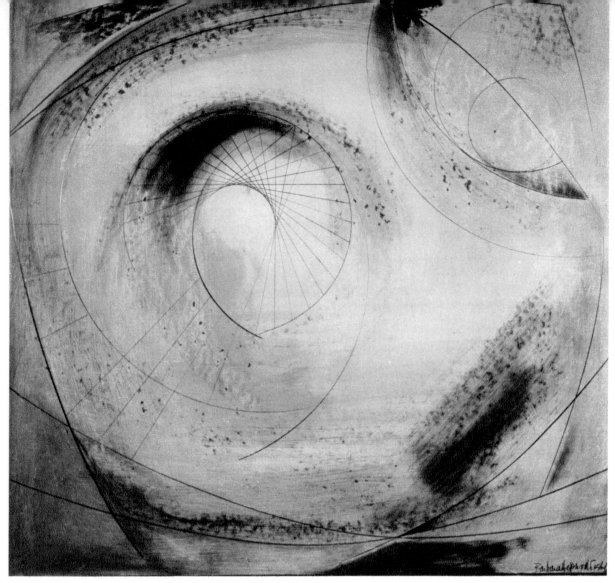

BARBARA HEPWORTH
Stone form (Mincarlo), 1961

BARBARA HEPWORTH
Seated girl (back view), 1949

years afterwards, from standing up for the short series of animated and fascinating works by Gaudier. He had intimate contacts with James Joyce and T.S. Eliot.

In these mixed modernist circles painting was represented by Wyndham Lewis (1882-1957) who was also a novelist. Together with Pound, Lewis published the periodical *Blast* which acquired much fame in its short life, but for all that was an outlet for the rebellious spirit. For some time Lewis was a cubist. The *Blast*-spirit deviated strongly from the Bloomsbury convictions over post-impressionism. *Blast* finally condemned the Greek dominant in art, it was opposed to the romantic anecdote, it was averse to passivity, a champion of motion, but it rejected the imitated motion of futurism. It paid attention to prehistory, the Aztecs, Shang and Chow (China). The whole movement became known under the name of Vortex, which, as vorticism, represented a programme of iconoclasts. It was Gaudier who in June 1914 wrote his confession of faith as regards sculpture under the title of *Gaudier-Brzeska-Vortex*. This document is still striking, rich in comment about the sculpture of Africa, Oceania, China, Greece and Mexico, and obviously influenced by what Gaudier had seen in Paris of the cubists, Brancusi and Zadkine. Coming from Gaudier in London, it struck a new and vigorous note about sculpture. It began as follows:

'Sculptural energy is the mountain
Sculptural feeling is the appreciation of masses in relation
Sculptural ability is the defining of these masses by planes. '

His own work was, as is often the case with a young man between twenty and twenty-three, unstable in quality and character.

Undeniably Epstein was too severe in his judgment of him, just as he had been with Zadkine. He said in his autobiography '. . . a picturesque slight figure with lively eyes, and a sprouting beard . . . Far from innovating, Gaudier always followed. He followed quickly, overnight as it were . . . We were interested in each other's work. '

This contains a germ of truth. Between a stylized figuration (*The Dancer*) and a vigorous cubist work, *The Hieratic Head of Ezra Pound* (1914), we find variants that show an archaic influence and make it impossible to predict what he would have produced later if death on the battlefield in France had not cruelly cut short this sensitive and enthusiastic life. Gaudier acted as a ferment in the English history of sculpture.

In this Jacob Epstein had preceded him in another way.

Epstein had come to Europe provided with a good training. He always remained grateful for what he was taught in his youth in New York by George Gray Barnard. In 1901 he worked in a bronze foundry. His years in Paris (1902-5) at the Ecole des Beaux-Arts and the Académie Julien were perhaps less important than his contact with the *avant-garde,* which was repeated in 1912, when he was in Paris to be present at the placing of Oscar Wilde's tomb, and met Brancusi, Modigliani, Picasso and Paul Guillaume. His voracious and extensive interest in archaic and exotic sculptures was amazing. He became a passionate collector, whose accumulation of objects could only be compared with Jacques Lipchitz' collection. When in 1960, after Epstein's death his collection was shown to the public, no less an expert than William Fagg wrote: 'This exhibition has been conceived in the first place as a foot-note to the art history of our time, a documentary exposition of the nature of Sir Jacob Epstein's always profound interest in the sculpture of other peoples and other times and thus a comment on the little-understood relationship between so-called "primitive art" and that of twentieth-century Europe.'

He made England conscious of the meaning of sculpture, and he was the first to start speaking of form in general. Every time Epstein achieved something for architecture—the Strand Statues (1907-8), destroyed in 1937 by the Rhodesian government, the sepulchral monument to Oscar Wilde (1912), the Rima Relief (Hudson Memorial, 1924)—and in free works of importance, a violent public reaction was the result. Leonard Woolf in his remarkable autobiography, *Beginning Again* says: 'The British middle class—and, as far as that goes, the aristocracy and working class —are incorrigibly philistine, and their taste is impeccably bad. Anything new in the arts, particularly if it is good, infuriates them and they condemn it as either immoral or ridiculous or both.' This commotion stirred up the press as well as the defenders. Nobody could be indifferent to it, but—as Henry Moore expressed it with warm gratitude (*Sunday Times*, 23 August, 1959)—the sculptor had to take the blows and swallow the insults in order to pave the way for the younger ones.

As a portraitist Epstein was given many commissions. These works caused his importance as an *avant-garde* artist and fighter in the Vortex period to be eventually forgotten by the younger generation.

But a number of important works were produced in the experimental period preceding 1914 (for instance the *Group of Birds* in alabaster and *Rock Drill,* 1913-14).

These *Birds* are clear-cut, tense volumes that may be seen in relation to Brancusi. Works made by Barbara Hepworth in her early days (birds) and by Henry Moore more than ten years later were probably not directly inspired by Epstein, but in this period Epstein was undeniably for a short time at a point quite close to abstract possibilities that were to be resumed with energy a generation later.

It may be said that *Rock Drill* became the symbol of vorticism. The modelling is severe, and clearly shows great tension. The theme cannot be seen unrelated to the lyrical interest in the machine that prevailed in those days. The writer-painter Wyndham Lewis, who advocated a style based on a passion for the machine, had already made abstract work that was

LYNN CHADWICK - *Study for 'relief' face,* 1961

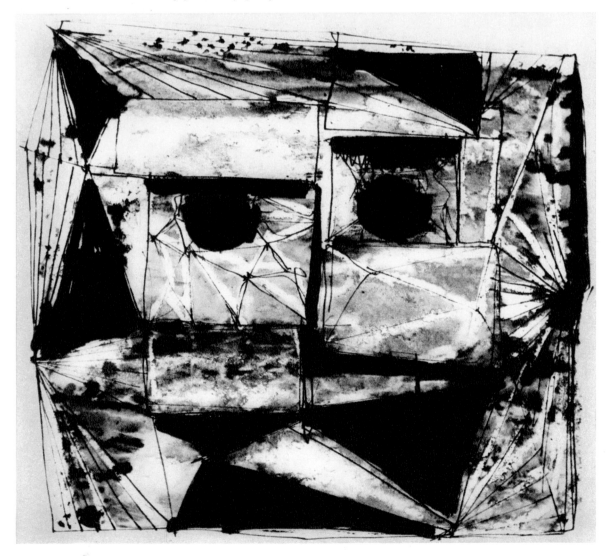

followed by a figurative cubism in which Robot Man appeared. 'Here is the armed, sinister figure of today and tomorrow. No humanity, only the terrible Frankenstein monster we have made ourselves into'. These are Epstein's words from his autobiography. Mechanized man is a phenomenon determined by a certain period in art. One has only to think of Léger's *Soldiers Playing Cards*.

With the portraits, Epstein continued a tradition which he had seen started by Rodin. Not blind to his faults, but less critical than Ricketts had been, he had a great admiration for Rodin's abundant production, his imagination and daring. Epstein made portraits of women, members of his family, and well-known personalities who, to his sorrow, only became his sitters when they were sufficiently famous and consequently old enough to be perpetuated in bronze. All of them are now denigrated more often than not, but the future will no doubt separate the chaff from the wheat and what will remain will be a number of magnificent heads which, due to the power of observation and expression, have carried on the line started by Rodin in his *Man with the Broken Nose*.

The secret of the portraits is not only to be found in his knowledge and ability, but especially in his liberal, warm and humane character open to the intrinsic nature of the human being in front of him. I think Moore expressed the exact truth, when he wrote after Epstein's death: 'He was an intensely warm man, who in his work transmitted that warmth, that vitality, that feeling for human beings immediately'. He was utterly free from the English reserve towards feelings, and perhaps it was this unrestricted, passionate self-surrender expressed in each separate work, that again and again called forth an English revolt caused by hurt conventionalism, prudishness and formality.

In his other works Epstein, having been fascinated by Brancusi, cubism, Egyptian and exotic forms, remained wavering. He shied away from limitations and bias, always innate in the act of abstraction. His talent and his great ability often led to problematical works in consequence of his dualistic attitude. But, despite this, his work has born fruit. He accomplished the hard but necessary task of pulling down the walls of English resistance and conventionalism. Not without bitterness Epstein, after many injurious attacks, came to the conclusion that England was after all becoming conscious of the three-dimensional form.

In literature there appeared an opposition to 'the passion for machines', as Aldous Huxley called it in his *Music at Night* (*The New Romanticism*). Intelligence and critical sense have not always sufficed to appreciate cubism, whose principle was made an issue by vorticism, and the lyricism of the machine. It was no great help that a man like Aldous Huxley, and many with him, ridiculed the movement: 'The Cubist dehumanization of art is frequently accompanied by a romantic and sentimental admiration for machines. Fragments of machinery are generously scattered through modern painting. There are sculptors, who laboriously try to reproduce the forms invented by engineers . . . The passion for machines, so characteristic of modern art, is a kind of regression to what I may call second boyhood.'

The first World War inflicted terrible wounds.

The deaths of Hulme and Gaudier on the battlefield of Flanders and France were a heavy loss for the *avant-garde* camp. D. H. Lawrence evoked the mental state in London in *Kangaroo*.

'It was in 1915 the old world ended. In the winter 1915-1916 the spirit of the Old London collapsed; the city, in some way, perished, perished from being the heart of the world, and became a vortex of broken passions, lusts, hopes, fears, and horrors. The integrity of London collapsed and the genuine debasement began, the unspeakable baseness of the press and the public voice, the reign of that bloated ignominy "John Bull".'

Nevertheless, in the world of sculpture an independent life had begun to stir among the English sculptors. The attention bestowed on Epstein and Gaudier, and subsequently on the development between 1920 and 1930 of Henry Moore and Barbara Hepworth, left some transitional English figures unintentionally overlooked. These proved in themselves that a peculiar insular life was being born. Leon Underwood (born 1890) is an example. As the result of numerous travels and an ardent interest in extra-European sculpture he not only made a practice of carving but also expressed, at an early date, the importance of a totally different modelling from that of the Renaissance. His profound knowledge and experience of exotic sculpture made him, as a writer on this subject, an authority who was recognized even in professional circles. As such, he deserves to be mentioned next to Carl Einstein who, raising his voice in Germany, was the first writer who recommended new plastic aesthetics based on the sculpture of Africa and Oceania. It is still to be decided to what extent Underwood, as a creative force preceding the generation of Henry Moore, should be considered a pioneer. It was Underwood who at the Royal College gave drawing-lessons to young Henry Moore. It is to be regretted that in his more recent work he has given up carving in exchange for figurative sculptures in bronze with lyrical themes that are rather expressionistic, but show structurally a weak romanticism.

The notion that sculpture could renew itself and create a stronger consciousness of form by abandoning modelling in clay or wax for carving in wood or stone found its supporters among those who wanted to restore the connection with architecture and achieve a monumental style. The free artists, less convinced of this monumental renaissance, also sympathized with the idea that the vindication of the form could invigorate sculpture more proficiently than Rodin had done by modelling in clay for the bronze foundries.

Thus England had a number of sculptors who reached an estimable average that was moderately modern in its conception of form and style, remaining at best somewhere on a level with Maillol. Eric Gill still had a background of the arts and crafts idea revived under the leadership of William Morris. Though endowed with a versatile talent, he remained in his relief sculpture for architecture archaically decorative in character. Refined, subtly intelligent, his work remained weak from a creative point of view. What he did for Oxford, Cambridge, and Guildford Cathedral was not innovatory. In another province (lettering) he did work of lasting importance.

Frank Dobson (born 1887) introduced something of Maillol's style into England, which was still acceptable to the circle of Fry and the Bloomsbury Group. He was also a supporter of the principle of direct carving.

Between 1920 and 1940 Eric Kennington was repeatedly mentioned in the art magazines. It is indicative of the moderate public interest and a modernized, but essentially conventional taste which yet again had become predominant after the first World War, that in the art magazines we regularly come across sculptors who have now fallen into the background. In 1939 a whole issue of *The Studio* was devoted to 'Sculpture of Today' with a text written by Stanley Casson M.A., in which Gill, Dobson, Epstein and Dobbington are the leading men, in which Milles, Rosandic and Mestrovic are still highly appreciated, and in which Henry Moore is mentioned as the maker of 'a number of lovely works' and as one who is going to found a 'school'.

Direct carving was a healthy method to achieve restoration, but it does not guarantee important creativity.

England had more sculpture than in the past, but in relative silence and obscurity some younger artists grew up who, though mature before 1940, could only after the second World War convince the world of an authentic English sculpture, important as a phenomenon on the international level

LYNN CHADWICK
Maquette for Two Winged Figures, 1955

14

and occupying an essential and dominating place in the plastic art of the twentieth century. They altered the image of English art. This time they did it not by causing a breach, but by the creative cultural power of which their work gave evidence.

Viewed officially, it might seem that between 1920 and 1940 a retrogression took place as a result of an increased semi-modern civilization, the adoration of a spurious pathos, heroism and virtuosity (Milles, Mestrovic, Rosandic). In reality an animated continuity of interchange between the Continent and the insular advanced artist had come into being. Unlike the days of Whistler, Steer and Sickert, it was an interchange that did not suffer from a continental supremacy. As Patrick Heron (in *The Changing Forms of Art,* London 1955) rightly observes: 'British art cannot indefinitely labour under the burden of inferiority with which it has been saddled by Roger Fry and his friends'. However, Fry's period was still one of the pictorial elements, against which Ricketts, who was not a good sculptor himself, but who was a man of great erudition, had given a sharp warning with regard to sculpture.

England was doing excellently in literature between 1910 and 1930. After 1930 some important figures drop away: Virginia Woolf, Lawrence, Joyce, Pound. It was between 1920 and 1930 that the foundations were laid of a fruitful English sculpture, drawing in the beginning—in Moore's and Barbara Hepworth's youth—from continental sources, but now with an original creative transformation, at first quite unknown to many. And again there was a writer, well versed in philosophical psychology, who, in direct contact with the development, grasped and gave expression to this new English world of the sculptural form, using the means of the carefully thought-out word, and placing it in comprehensive conjunction with creative and psychical values. After Fry, Ezra Pound and Hulme, Herbert Read became not so much the interpreter as the accompanist, establishing himself as the mediator between the artist and the public, stimulating and intensifying the sensations. Like Moore and Barbara Hepworth, Read has gained an international reputation. Studies not only show that he was a sensitive observer, but also that, closely following the creative activities of painters and sculptors, he consequently found the elements with which he built up his own vision and aesthetic principles. The high level and the methods of English aesthetics and criticism, which are for instance manifest in the studies of Douglas Cooper (*Klee, De Staël, Léger, Braque* and his volume on the Courtauld Collection), in the striking dissertations written by Kenneth Clark, the psycho-aesthetically important reflections on art of Adrian Stokes, and in the work of the critics of the *Burlington Magazine,* may well serve as an example to other countries. However, in this respect Read is no art critic, but a poetically philosophical interpreter (or accompanist), who is deeply attached to the art of his generation, and who, especially in regard to sculptural consciousness, has done valuable work.

The sculptural birth, taking place between 1920 and 1940 more or less below the surface of official interest and appreciation, should not be seen as a phenomenon isolated from a kindred orientation and fructification in painting. Ben Nicholson (born 1894) played an important part in this respect. He underwent the influence of vorticism as late as 1918, thus proving its connection, though only by a thin thread, with his own development and that of Moore and Hepworth between 1920 and 1930. When afterwards, in 1921, he saw work by Picasso in Paris, he became conscious of cubism. But it is probable that his susceptibility to this great impression was activated by elements that had come to him from vorticism and the work of Wyndham Lewis. His attitude towards art may also be inferred from his choice of artists whose work attracted him. From 1925 to 1936 he was a member of the Seven and Five Group, composed of seven painters and five sculptors, who already in 1919 rebelled against the

Bloomsbury dictatorship, which through Fry's influence had succeeded in getting the neo-impressionist values accepted as 'the advocates of modern art', but was blind to other values that came later. To the Seven and Five Group belonged, among others, John Piper, Christopher Wood, Henry Moore and Barbara Hepworth. Attention originally directed towards surrealism was turned aside by Ben Nicholson in the direction of abstraction. Nicholson developed an exclusive interpretation of cubism and purely abstract values which from then on made it impossible to speak of an art deriving from France, as had been the case with Lewis. This was an individual and at the same time English creative revelation. His starting point was painting, which towards the end of 1933 was extended to a particular kind of carved and coloured relief. The relief originated in an extremely subtle and exact type of spatial feeling, which is treated by some as part of sculpture, though it rather belongs to the art of collage which since the rise of cubism has become so rich in varieties. It is a special kind of art that, with the plane as the starting-point of spatial

HENRI GAUDIER-BRZESKA - *Seated woman*, c. 1912

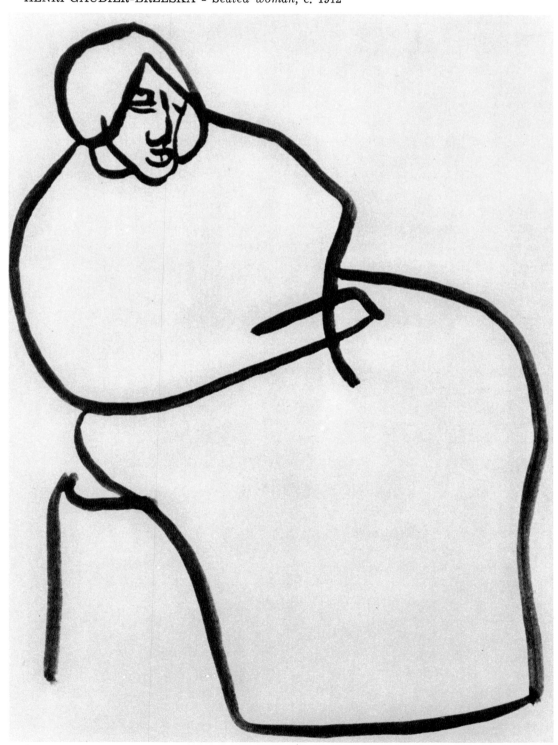

feeling, treats space with a great reserve. It is a phenomenon that has all sorts of ramifications, starting from Mondrian and continuing in Pasmore, Baljeu, Biederman and present-day constructivism. There is a connection between the development of English pictorial abstraction in Nicholson and the development of English sculpture in its reaction to landscape and emotional abstraction.

This is the moment to remember another isolated fact which demonstrates the sense of abstraction awakening in England, and which was moreover the first direct link between England and Mondrian.

Marlow Moss (1890-1958) had a hard and solitary life, struggling with her family and struggling to free her artistic personality, living and working in London and Cornwall alternately until in 1927 she discovered work by Mondrian in Paris. In immediate contact with Mondrian and very much under his magnetic influence, she elaborated his principle, but with a personal accent. She settled in France and stayed there, until the war utterly destroyed her house and her work. In 1941, robbed of her production, and back again in Cornwall, she started doing three-dimensional work. She continued to develop her own ideas, without any contact with the Nicholson-Hepworth-Moore group though she was familiar with their work. She also lived and worked in the Netherlands (on the Isle of Walcheren), where she was known only in the circle around the novelist Mrs A. H. Nijhoff, who later became her biographer.

A momentous occurrence in this whole development that was to be carried through later by Moore and Barbara Hepworth was the publication of the book *Circle,* shortly before the surrealist and the constructively abstract trends were to separate. It was preceded by the book *Unit One* published by the group of the same name, founded in 1934.

Circle provided in word and image, untroubled by the phraseology of manifestoes, an account of the work of a number of English and Continental artists and how they conceived the world would be as seen from London. It described a collective atmosphere and demonstrated the oneness of architecture, sculpture and painting, free from surrealism which had been held on close terms with abstraction by the Seven and Five Group and Unit One. Two years later, when the great hurricane burst out over Europe, the majority of the foreigners had left for America, a fact which the English deplored.

Thus the years from 1931 to 1937 were decisive years of great activity, with an intensive interchange of ideas between England and the European Continent sustained by a group of congenial painters, sculptors and architects. After having established the importance of the spiritual interchange in England between 'displaced' architects and the English artists, let us now turn our attention to the more incidental but no less fruitful visits which Ben Nicholson paid to Europe, first alone, and later (after 1932) together with Barbara Hepworth. In 1932: Picasso, Braque, Brancusi, Jean Arp, Sophie Täuber-Arp; 1933: Brancusi again, Mondrian, Jean Helion, Herbin; 1935: Mondrian and Naum Gabo; 1936: Calder, Miró, Braque, Arp. These visits took place twenty years after Epstein, in 1912, had met Brancusi, Picasso, Modigliani and others in the early period of cubism. It cannot be doubted that Brancusi made an impression, perhaps more so than the others, but to Epstein the effect was not lasting. He did not recognize the profound and significant influence of foreign travel on the younger ones of 1930. He said the influence was too great and banal, it had become popular, and was even to be seen in Regent Street shops.

Henry Moore's travels gained importance when in 1925 he visited Rome, Florence, Pisa, Siena, Assisi, Padua and Venice. In 1936 he went to Spain and saw the prehistoric works of art in Altamira; and he visited Toledo, Madrid and Barcelona. But already in 1921 Moore went in search of sculptures by paying repeated visits to the treasures of the British Museum,

BARBARA HEPWORTH - *Vertical forms*, 1951

visits that were at least as important as his later travels. It is a remarkable fact that during the period of Moore's artistic development, the impressions of the styles prevalent in the great cultural eras in and outside Europe were more important to him than the more individual contacts with the artists of his own time, though in the circle round Nicholson-Hepworth these artists were of supreme importance. Deeply impressed by Mexican sculpture, Henry Moore established a direct connection with the eleventh-century sculpture which he had seen, when a child, in the churches of Yorkshire. Passionately he included the historical in the present, not from the experience of knowledge, but as a creative act, resulting from an intense vision. Continually he referred to the fact that a work must have 'vitality of its own' and 'an intense life of its own, independent of the object it may represent', that it must be 'self-supporting', 'fully in the round'.

Something of Gaudier's Vortex slogans can be heard in Moore's *A View*

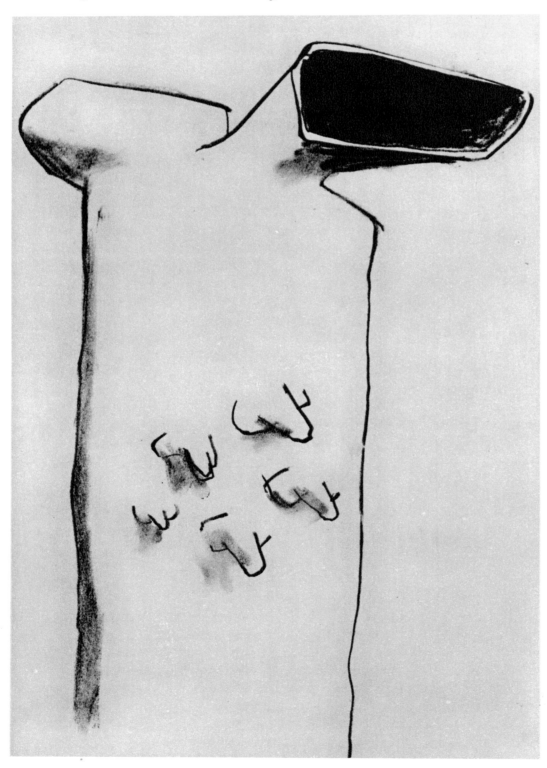

KENNETH ARMITAGE - *Drawing (Pandarus series)*, 1963

20

of Sculpture when he demands that sculpture should be 'strong, vital, giving out something of the energy and power of great mountains' (see *A View of Sculpture,* 1930, and *The Sculptor's Aims,* 1934). In 1934, he formulated a demand, highly characteristic, potentially conflicting and consequently a source of tension: '... abstract qualities of design are essential to the value of a work, but to me of equal importance is the psychological human element. If both abstract and human elements are welded together in a work, it must have a fuller, deeper meaning.'

From the standpoint of this conviction, he views the great archaic cultures of the world. This point of view determines his relation to nature, to rocks, trees, shells and bones. From this point of view it can be understood why elements of landscape and of man live on in a changed form in his vital world of forms, altered into a magically sensed life of matter. Closely connected with this is what he expects of the forces slumbering in matter. This is not only important to Moore himself, but also of interest when one tries to understand the reaction to it in the younger ones, who, as his pupils and assistants, came under the spell—how could it be otherwise?—of his world of forms and thoughts, and who afterwards tried, often in vain, to escape from it, and to vindicate their own point of view. 'Truth to material' which had become a slogan, was set forth by Moore in 1934 in the following words: 'Every material has its own individual qualities. It is only when the sculptor works direct, when there is an active relationship with his material, that the material can take its part in the shaping of an idea.'

'Constructive Art' became the connecting idea, and in 1935 it gave rise to the suggestion of a publication. This was developed in the studio of Ben Nicholson and Barbara Hepworth, together with Naum Gabo and the architect J. L. Martin and his wife. It was published by Faber & Faber in July 1937. The editors were J. L. Martin, Ben Nicholson and Naum Gabo, and its title was *Circle - International Survey of Constructive Art.* It was the condensation of the ideas emerging from conversations between the English artists and the European architects and artists who had fled to London: Gropius, Breuer, Mendelssohn, Gabo, Moholy-Nagy. In *Circle,* Gabo dominated. Herbert Read, Mondrian, Lewis Mumford, Karel Honzig, the scientist J. D. Bernal, Henry Moore, Maxwell Fry, Le Corbusier, Barbara Hepworth and Walter Gropius were among the contributors. Various new styles of architecture from foreign countries were shown. Mondrian arrived from Paris in 1938. He held his authoritative position in the Circle not through his argumentativeness but through his very presence. His studio, transformed by himself, was opposite the Nicholson-Hepworth studio in Hampstead, where Moore and Herbert Read were also living. *Circle* has become a valuable epochal document, symbolizing a pre-war moment in the development of abstraction, in which already firmly shaped convictions in the minds of artists found each other, while surrounded by the menace of war.

The introduction by the editors began as follows:

'A new cultural unity is slowly emerging out of the fundamental changes which are taking place in our present-day civilization ... In starting this publication we have a dual purpose; firstly to bring this work before the public, and secondly, to give the artists—painters, sculptors, architects and writers—the means of expressing their views and of maintaining contact with each other. Our aim is to gather here those forces which seem to us to be working in the same direction and for the same ideas, but which are, at the moment, scattered, many of the individuals working on their own account and lacking any medium for the interchange of ideas.'

The intuitive acceptance of limits and potential forces in matter, which take part in the formative process that precedes the birth of the image, was the logical conclusion resulting from the 'direct carving' idea. This idea, directed against modelling in clay and drawing-room sculpture, came into being when, together with the Gothic revival, the conviction was re-established that sculptures to be included in architecture required a different conception as well as a different, that is to say medieval, procedure. This monumentality, based on architecture, had been brought to a standstill when architecture and sculpture drifted apart. Therefore Moore consistently stands up for 'direct carving' and the 'truth to material' idea in free sculpture. He demands truth and character in the work, not beauty according to the rules fixed by Hellenistic aesthetics. '"Beauty" in the later Greek or Renaissance sense is not the aim in my sculpture ... Like beauty, true simplicity is an unselfconscious virtue; it comes by the way and can never be an end in itself' (*The Listener*, 24 April, 1941).

Keenly sensible of the importance of the unconscious, of surrealism, of the 'non-logical', Moore has always paid tribute to the fullness of the personality; he considered conscious control and the force of domination just as indispensable as the jostling, conflicting forces. Though in 1936 Moore exhibited work together with a surrealist group (to which Paul Nash also belonged), it is in my opinion too far-fetched to look upon this fact as significant. The real surrealism, as it was led by the two adversaries Tzara and Breton, with all the developments inherent in it, such as automatism, occultism, and so on, and as it manifested itself powerfully in the work of Max Ernst, Dali, Delvaux and Giacometti, is not to be found in Moore. As his mind was open to his own time, as he was not afraid of seriously studying what others did, surrealism naturally engaged his attention, but it never became an essential element in his creations.

It is thanks to this centripetal force of a complex, emotional personality which lets the fullness of life with all its elements participate in his work that Henry Moore's animation of the form possesses such a strong emanation, and has such a vast influence. In point of fact it is the orchestration of a scale of forms under the conductorship of the final unity of his inner personality. The contradictions which are present within him he does not show as such; he exorcizes them.

In a certain sense he summarizes, and consequently he finds a rich response. His work is comparable only with that of his older contemporary Lipchitz, in which form and motives, abstraction and figuration, determine the emotional, reactive tensions, but which, by expressing itself exclusively in bronze, though certainly with an unsurpassed experience and command of the technique, has not brought out the relation to stone and wood, as is so strikingly the case with Moore.

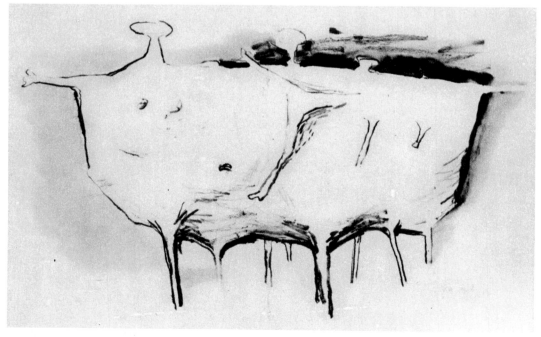

KENNETH ARMITAGE - *Standing Group*, 1958

The reaction of the younger artists, most respectfully opposed to Moore's domination, is quite the reverse of the reaction of the younger artists of 1910 to Rodin. Every domination evokes in the psychological and aesthetic domain the forces that seek a correspondence between their own time and their creative intentions which differ from the one represented in the figure of the father. However, the 'truth to material' idea, which was lacking in Rodin and is, objectively seen, a universal power in Moore, has undergone certain corrections.

Barbara Hepworth, too, discovered, after years of a puritan clinging to 'direct carving' in wood, marble or stone, the freer possibilities of bronze (1956) but with a personal technique, which moreover contains a secondary direct tooling of the bronze by the artist (J.P. Hodin gives a description of this technique in the monograph on Barbara Hepworth, Neuchâtel 1961). There still remains an enormous difference between the bronzes of Rodin and his adherents, based on modelled clay figures, and the technique of working in plaster, which also permits direct carving—a technique later also applied by Moore, when he did not abandon carving but turned to the use of bronze. John Russell (Marlborough Fine Arts, London, 1961) brilliantly analyzed the bronzes in Moore's work, as opposed to the carvings, after A.D.B. Sylvester in 1951, on the occasion of the Tate Gallery Exhibition, had raised with sensitive intelligence the question of the fundamental differences between the modelled figures and the carved ones in the years 1922-30.

It was also Russell who pointed out that the influence exercised by the frescoes of Masaccio and Michelangelo (the cartoon in the British Museum) was limited to the naturalistic tradition in modelled sculpture, and who postulated the influence of pre-Columbian and other extra-European styles on the carvings. The impression which Masaccio made was a temporary phenomenon. It became perceptible when in 1924 Barbara Hepworth, aged twenty-one, made a trip to Italy and admired in Florence Masaccio's majestically monumental figures. And the same applied to the young Moore who travelled in Italy a year later.

We can now look back over more than forty years of Moore's work. It has grown along with the century; the opposite is also true. Yet the reason why the evolution in his work came about in this way and not differently is to be found in a few principles rooted in his inner and creative life. What he gathered in from the outside world was much: the extra-European sculptures, especially in their archaic periods; church sculpture in Yorkshire seen in his childhood; in Europe the work of Picasso, Arp and Giacometti; Masaccio from the Renaissance and also something of Michelangelo; from nature: shells, bones, rocks, caves and, to a somewhat lesser degree, Man.

In the years between 1922 and 1934 this inexhaustible world in which his sculptor's eye and heart lived became visible. Not all at once, but with a certain rhythm, the principal accents of his discoveries in the world of art outside himself made themselves felt. It was a blending of many forms taken from nature and from culture, but it was also a choice, determined by what was already present in Moore, and which became conscious by means of intuition and instinct. In the same period, motives make their appearance; they are all-embracing, universal. As motives they mean nothing to Moore but a different method by which to awaken what is potentially present in the most impenetrable regions of his being. The motives are half figures, mother and child, the recumbent woman, the family group, heads of animals, helmeted heads, forms parallel with the shapes of nature (organic abstractions). Erich Neumann in particular wrote about the archetypes and their symbolic significances in Moore's work. Moore has always avoided adding anything literary or symbolic to his images in their titles, though they offer every opportunity for applying evocative romantic titles, calling up Ossian-like landscapes, primeval figures, genetic visions.

Moore lets his images speak for themselves, without mythical or other appellations. And he is always exact, so with changes in his work different titles appear which are invariably factual. In 1931 the abstract title of 'Composition' starts to make its appearance, though as yet only rarely; in 1932 abstract titles increase in number, and in 1933 they predominate, to become the rule between 1934 and 1937 as 'Sculpture', 'Carving', 'Two Forms', 'Square Form'. In 1938-39 they give way to 'Stringed Figure', to return in 1939-40 to human titles such as 'Family Group', 'Madonna and Child' and 'Reclining Figure'.

Werner Hofmann has tried to explain the English character of this plastic art by means of an astute search for comparable characteristics in old English stone crosses, Anglo-Saxon book illuminations and the work of William Blake (see *Henry Moore - Schriften und Skulpturen,* 1959, Fischer Bucherei). He might also have mentioned romantic traits (for instance *The Sleeping Knights* by Burne Jones, with torsos like that of Moore's *Warrior*).

However, in all these estimates we are continually worried by a feeling that after all something is escaping us, that something has remained unsaid.

Of course Moore has deep roots in his native country and also in his own time, with the result that a wide-spread root system has come into existence, within himself and in the world outside. What goes on nourishing this sculpture remains to a considerable extent hidden from the eye. As he himself consciously repels in his titles what his critical, literary and psychoanalytical commentators want to bring out, we feel obliged to respect his wish, and to confine ourselves to the forms and motives.

These forms give in the course of their development a powerful image of what sculpture can be in our time. One might say that these universal motives and forms encircle the sculptor himself, so that he becomes subjected to his own creations, undergoes them, and, in order to escape from them, starts working on them again, re-creates them, only to discover that, as one gets older, not only one's reactions to the things made by others count, but also one's own reactions to the things one made oneself. Because of this the artist's world becomes more complex. Old motives return, they are formed anew, and at the same time they prove the inescapable character of the energy of the primitive motives deeply rooted in his being. The fact that he is doomed to exist only in and through sculpture is made bearable by the triumph of being able to change, to re-create an earlier 'motive' in new subjects, or to discover new motives in a single subject.

When we consider the earliest 'reclining figures' of Moore in 1926-27, it can be seen that the motive is the same as that successfully made in bronze by Epstein in his best years, just as Epstein in his motives of alabaster birds in a severe style anticipated Moore's treatment of the motive of a dog in marble in 1922 and of the powerful and simple motive of a snake in 1924. It is still in the vortex atmosphere.

The 'reclining figures' return in 1929-30 in a full and large volume, which in its fluent forms is slightly suggestive of a Maillol-Dobson style, but which in the 'Reclining Woman' in green Hornton stone (National Gallery of Canada, Ottawa) is transformed into a much more powerful, imposing and austere formula to arrive in 1934 startlingly at a magnificent abstraction in African wonderstone.

It is a metamorphosis of the old feminine motive, in which the curves of the volume are retained, but in which the form approaches that of a vertebra. Into the old motive a second one has crept. The subject remains the same, but the form, the style of the subject, is a welding of two motives.

Here and elsewhere the concept 'motive' is used in the sense defined by Sir Kenneth Clark in his remarkable lecture under the title of *Motives*, delivered in New York in 1961 (20th International Congress of the History of Art).

In this we touch the secret of the abstraction in Moore's work. There has been some talk of a certain distortion of the natural appearance. As a matter of fact, it is a mistake ever to speak of distortions in Moore's work. What takes place is a fusion of motives in his potency as a sculptor. This fusion causes the human figure and the organic forms of nature (shells, bones) to blend, with the result that there appears an autonomous form, a third form, that is neither an abstraction of the one nor of the other, nor a distortion, but an authentic sculptor's form. The 'reclining figures' reappear at intervals. When for the moment we ignore many transformations, we see in 1934 the birth of *Two Forms* in wood and a *Four-piece composition: reclining figure* in Cumberland alabaster. Superficially seen: absolute abstraction, a connection of loose objects to which belongs a body with curved planes and with a precisely formed hole, which, protectively, absorbingly bends over a much smaller stylized volume that belongs to it but has no physical relationship with it.

Now taking a long stride towards recent days, we again find the 'reclining figures' with a large number of intermediate variations in 1961-62, more than thirty-five years after they first made their appearance. This time Moore has hewn the large figures, conceived in bronze, in two or three pieces. They rise like rocks, stones dating from a prehistoric era, and lie like parts of a landscape in a landscape.

Looking back on 1934 we see that already in those days, filled with a craving for abstraction, Moore had essentially fixed it all in a supreme unity of matter, form and subject—the mystery of the pierced volume, the curved forms, the darkness of caverns and the tension in the space between severed parts that belong together because of their relationship, from the smaller to the bigger, from the spherical to the hollow, from what is reclining to what rises. But in 1934 the fusion bore the sign of the time: the crystal, the complete achievement. In 1961 it is the rugged form, the suggestion of corrosion, the romanticism, in the deepest and grandest sense of the word, of the majestic landscape belonging to prehistoric times, which in the cellars of our minds is waiting for the return into the light. It is a continual rebirth of motives which, once created, continue living in Moore's mind, and which for ever want to extend their power as a form-creating energy over him, trying again and again to ascertain who is the stronger. And no sooner had these primeval mountains of women left his workshop than Moore once more showed the miracle of the renewal within himself and the connection with the things of the past.

In 1962 are born the curious *Knife-edge: two-piece* and the *Locking piece*, reminding one of ancient Chinese bronzes. They are forms like the bones of imaginary beings, organic abstractions related to an earlier motive but now, owing to size, material and treatment of the surface, more rugged, more mysterious and fuller, as if another motive had joined in. They are authentic sculptors' forms, not natural, not human, not abstract; forms out of a third world, the world of the sculptors.

It is possible to write various essays on Moore. One finds three separate stories or histories of development—the 'interior and exterior' form, the principle of piercing the volume (the holes) and the principle of the stringed forms. All three of them are essentials in Moore's work. When we place them in the context of European sculpture, it becomes clear that all three of them are based on the possibilities produced by cubism.

In England it may be disputed whether Henry Moore or Barbara Hepworth was the first in 1931 to pierce the volume, to use the hole as an element of sculpture, but in fact it was Lipchitz who, in 1916, without

25

any logical inducement pierced the cubistic form for the first time. Archipenko stylized the holes indicated by the natural structure of the body. Brancusi used the closed volume. In 1925-28 Lipchitz made the next move in the direction of an entirely open sculpture with his 'transparent sculptures' which, as he thought in bronze, were based on the bronze technique, but were continued by others in wire.

Neither Moore nor Barbara Hepworth abandoned volume. They both opened the volume, but there is a subtle though clear difference in the character of the tunnels. The opening of these in the concave and convex forms propagated by cubism induced Moore to invent strings. Especially important in Moore's work are the interior and the exterior forms. The notion of the importance of the interior of a piece of sculpture also played a prominent part in Lipchitz' work in 1929-30, and turned up again and again: the garden figure of 1926-30, the *Song of the Vowels* (1931-32), the helmet-like head (1932), the studies for Notre Dame de Liesse (1950). Repeatedly they bestow an emphatic shape on the hollow, which seems to ask for a fruit, an interior. The themes of Mother and Child and the Prodigal Son encouraged him in this direction.

Henry Moore has found for the problem which with him is intertwined with the primitive motives of maternity and mother and child and the helmet motives, a solution covering the whole range from the human character to the organic abstraction. This solution was only possible because he never lost sight of the importance of the volume, and the opening, the hollow, was always felt in connection with the closing, the fullness, the protective. As a result the volume was charged internally with its own form, which, viewed in the light of the development of European sculpture, is in fact a synthesis of the available possibilities.

Barbara Hepworth is five years younger than Moore. She had, especially in the early years, identical sources of training (Leeds, the Royal College, a West Riding scholarship) and periods of travel in Europe (Italy and Paris). For her, too, 'truth to material' and 'direct carving' are fundamental rules, and they remained so even when she started to use bronze as a medium. Now that we are able to survey her work over a period of nearly forty years, we are struck by the fact that in the varying tensions between the involvement with landscape and the human being on the one hand and abstraction on the other, the leaning towards abstraction always preponderates, organic in nature but with an unmistakable inclination to the geometrical.

The magnificent retrospective exhibition which Bryan Robertson, in 1962, organized at the Whitechapel Art Gallery with devoted care, was convincing in this respect. It is moreover confirmed by a statement which the artist made herself:

'I think that the necessary equilibrium between the material I carve and the form I want to make will always dictate an abstract interpretation in my sculpture, for there are essential stone shapes and essential wood shapes which are impossible for me to disregard. All my feeling has to be translated into this basic framework, for sculpture is the creation of a *real object* which relates to our human body and spirit as well as our visual appreciation of form and colour content.'

So with Hepworth the abstraction is essentially different from Moore's. In fact it is questionable whether one should speak of absolute abstraction in Moore's work, even in the 1930s. The emotional reactions to the human figure and the landscape, expressing themselves in the motives that are rooted in his subconscious, became forms which nearly always, in their proportions, in the treatment of the surface, in the hollowing of the volume, retained a certain motion—a motion that is decidedly not without a dramatic element. The verticals appear and culminate in the *Three Upright Motives* that act magically and archaically in the landscape. Yet there is a dominant in the work of the reclining and seated figures (the

BARBARA HEPWORTH - *Enfant, 1929*

latter extended to the typically English motive of *The King and Queen*).
If Moore puts them against walls, one is inevitably forced to think of
earlier similar problems in the works of the Italian Arturo Martini. The
relationship is not so strange, because in Martini too there lived a dramatic tendency, more exuberant of course than in the more self-possessed
Moore, who would never lapse into cheap pathos, which Martini in his
later less brilliant years, could not escape.

There is even a link with the frescoes of Giotto in these figures, seated,
reclining or standing in front of walls, these figures that evoke an experience, an occurrence, because they are put in a clear relationship with
the walls. Another, and particularly with Moore not at all inconceivable,
connection is the burial-vault of Cerveteri, where the reliefs of the objects of life give a plastic rhythm to the walls.

When we return to Barbara Hepworth, we can see the motives of reclining figures, but the dominant inclines to the vertical. This she confirms
herself: 'The forms which have had a special meaning for me since childhood have been the standing forms (which is the translation of my feeling
towards the human being standing in landscape); the two forms (which is
the tender relationship of one living thing beside another); and the closed
form, such as the oval, spherical or pierced form (sometimes incorporating
a column), which translates for me the association and meaning of gesture
in landscape . . .'.

The standing form (she does not use the word 'figure'), the two forms and
the closed form are the three principal groups, in which a number of
motives found their basis. After a superficial inspection one might think
of an influence exercised by Gabo at the time when constructivism acted
as a magnet also setting the fashion in *Circle*. I have already mentioned
that Barbara Hepworth did not relinquish volume, but, together with
Henry Moore, approached transparent sculpture with the necessary reserve, without going as far as open wire constructions. But at times she
went quite a long way in the direction of open sculpture. The grand piece
of work for State House in London is a monumental example of this. The
other principles of constructivism did not influence her. The tradition of
wood, stone and marble and the very old English tradition of carving in
alabaster were continued by Hepworth, which was utterly at variance with
Gabo and Pevsner. As with Arp, working in plaster thoroughly disgusted
her, and the new materials that to her are no more than dead matter
(plexiglass, aluminium, etc), and which are recommended by the construc-
tivists, are useless to her. The principle of 'direct carving', revised perhaps but maintained in essence, is connected with this, and is of course
totally incompatible with Gabo's conception of sculpture.

During her trip to Italy, her teacher Ardini taught her 'direct carving',
which convinced her of the importance of the individual treatment of the
material. John Skeaping, whom she married during this Italian journey,
was, and still is, a much respected sculptor, who advocated the principle
as a wholesome tradition. When in 1930-32 she made the acquaintance
of Ben Nicholson's paintings, and of the already influential artist himself,
new possibilities were revealed to her. The relationship of their intentions, and the famous visits to Arp and Brancusi, caused a change of direction in her work. In fact certain elements in the work by the triumvi-
rate Nicholson-Arp-Brancusi were infused into her own sculptures. Though
she was a member of the Seven and Five Group, not a vestige of surrealism can be discovered in her work.

After her divorce from John Skeaping she married Ben Nicholson, and,
stimulated by association with the artists who had escaped from Nazi
Germany, abstraction was carried through energetically. The reliefs which
Ben Nicholson made as a painter, especially in 1934-39, greatly influenced
her own production, so that a fruitful interchange of ideas had started,
rare in the history of art, but perhaps comparable with the relationship

between Arp and Sophie Täuber, and that between Sonja Terk and Delaunay.

The use of colour in Barbara Hepworth's work since 1938 remains unique. In his *Dialogues on Art,* Edouardo Roditi relates how during the war an exploding bomb unearthed an Anglo-Norman capital, and how Barbara Hepworth then discovered that hollow parts had been covered with a 'bright terracotta red' which was exactly what she had been seeking since 1938 for her own work. At times the blues, greys, yellows and whites impart the image of the colour to the forms, which by this process are led back to their original motive—the motive that contains the energy which induces the artist to make his image in a certain way. Here is no question of a decorative colouring of the form, but in fact an evocation, via the chromatic emotion, of the original vision (occasionally in connection with the sea, the light, the beach, the surf).

Another important element is the surface treatment of the material, which is in fact the most personal and intimate element in the objective forms of her sculptures. It is the skin of the wood, the marble or the alabaster that appeals to the sense of touch. It is this contact which, with closed eyes, can still evoke a sensory and even a visual image. It embraces a complete scale of emotions, from the tenderness of a caress to the repugnance of a rough surface.

The strings are an intermediate world; as geometrical lines, tautly stretched, they appeal to the love of lucidity and transparency of mathematical thinking as well as to the fingertips that play the stringed instruments. Barbara Hepworth has developed this transparent possibility with great consistency, even in the monumental sculpture on the façade of the John Lewis building in Oxford Street.

Once, writing about her impressions of Brancusi, she said that his conception of the timeless elements of sculpture came very close to 'Stravinsky's understanding of rhythm'. 'They are elements, which belong to the primeval forces activating man's sensibilities; but they are, at the same time, sophisticated in the sense that they apprehend contemporary needs and passions, and re-affirm the continuity of life.'

Even since romanticism has been doing its utmost to efface the boundaries between the arts, it has been dangerous to transfer the world of music to that of painting or sculpture in a terminology in which the time element of music is no longer distinguished in the spatial element of sculpture. In his essay on Barbara Hepworth, J.P. Hodin laid particular stress on the classical Greek character of her work, not as a result of the Greek journey she made in 1954, but as the consequence of the innate ingenuity of her mind. This journey had no direct results, but it had an intense aftereffect. It seems to me that the abstraction in sculpture evoked by cubism and realized by the De Stijl movement in Holland was certainly not the fruit of a cultural stage comparable with the Greek 'abstract' style, which only in a preliminary stage, in the Cyclades, showed an advanced but by no means absolute abstraction, and was for the rest the reverse.

Equilibrium, clarity, simplicity are qualities of the mind that present themselves in figuration and abstraction.

What occurs in Barbara Hepworth's motives, loaded with energy, which precedes the image, is life itself; present, general and individual life with its emotions, tensions and impressions of the world, the landscapes and the seasons. It is a combination of contradictions and conflicts which, however, amalgamate in the sublime final form, in which light and shade, the spiral, the tunnel, an engraved line and a slight curve have reached a temporary agreement, an animated agreement, culminating in being still, in being vertical, in being pure. The mystery of clarity, the mystery of the inscrutable eye, which had been a closed depth in a large, grand and universal form like a shield, was ultimately pierced, transmitting the light like an eye in Barbara Hepworth's memorial to Dag Hammarskjöld, the deeply lamented Secretary of the United Nations Organization. In 1964, this work was placed near the UNO building on the East River in New York.

During the abstract period from 1932-44, her titles are factual and geometrical (*Form, Conoid, Helicoid, Two Forms, Single Forms, Carving, Pierced Hemisphere*). To these are added the secondary titles that refer to landscapes, to memories of Greece, or to a reaction to political occurrences (*Pelagos, Delos, Corinthos, Gothic, Menhirs, Orpheus, Aegean, Helios, Nyanga, Serena, Anima, Porthmeor, Trenona*). They are important because they reveal something of the origin and the content of the motives—contents which have a mixed character, and which are with Barbara Hepworth the key to the landscapes that are definable neither by painting nor by literature, but are sensations full of human feeling and take a sculptural form, which is autonomous.

The second World War cut the English community off from Western Europe, and the artists from the contact with the *Ecole de Paris*. In Cornwall the war once again made the insular spirit conscious of its own forces, but by that time the fight was already over.

The years before the war, the 1930s, years of a laborious and poor life, were the formative years, full of the spiritual power stronger than death, loaded with energy, able to stand up against the darkest trials of war as well as the trials of liberation, imminent prosperity and success.

When, after 1945, the work of Moore and Barbara Hepworth could be shown in Venice, Paris and elsewhere, it was the fruit of what had been sown and had grown before the war; the powerful poetry of sculpture, proceeding from the riches of the human mind and from the character of the landscape.

Continuation by the younger generation

It is inconceivable that the older artists would see without pain how the principles on behalf of which they had struggled and suffered were challenged, altered or abandoned by the younger ones. It was quite conceivable that the younger ones would develop what had been achieved, so that for the first time in England it might have been possible to speak of a 'school'. But this formation of a school hardly occurred in the meaning we attach to it. When we speak of an English School it is only a bit of slovenly parlance, but quite useful nevertheless. What is scholastic in it is not in the first place English; on the contrary, this sculpture is different from that of Western Europe and America in that it is so little 'schoolish' (to coin a word). Only in the work of Chadwick, Butler, and Armitage can be seen phenomena that render a use of the words 'English School' justifiable.

The sculptor Kenneth Martin still belongs to the generation of Barbara Hepworth (he was born in 1905) but owing to his late abstraction and afterwards his occupation with motion sculpture, he belongs to a more recent development. Incited by Calder's example but choosing his own field (birds and insects), Lynn Chadwick in his early days occupied himself before Martin with the problem of motion. But by about 1952 he abandoned mobiles.

Kenneth Martin, who was trained in Sheffield and at the Royal College of Art, and who became known as a painter (particularly of landscapes) started his abstract work between 1946-49, and in 1951 began to develop the spatial problem of motion. He is practically the only one in England who has persevered in this consistently in a wholly personal (one is tempted to say, delicate, pure and introvert) manner. He states himself: 'I have always liked the mobile for its possibilities of the profound non-seriousness'. But this non-seriousness is full of deep and semi-scientific meditations. He forms a contrast to Schöffer of Paris, who with the machine and

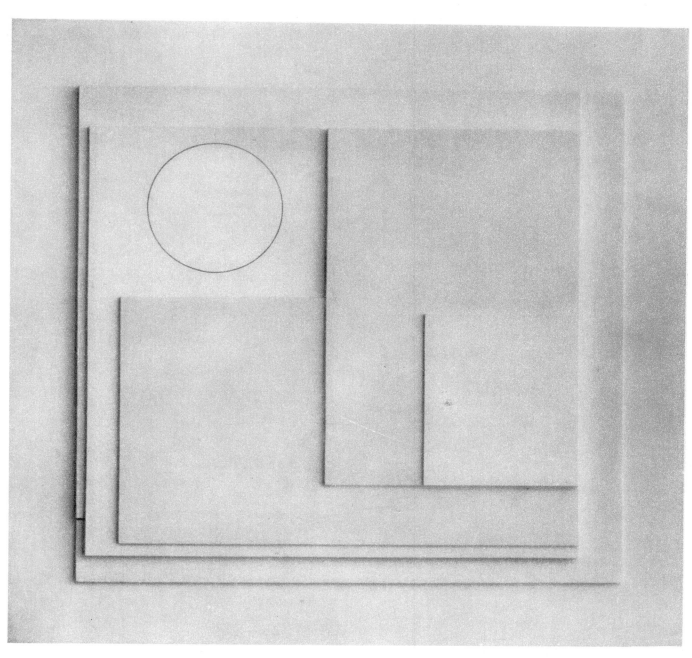

BEN NICHOLSON - *White Relief*, 1938

the newest electronic appliances, developed the possibility of motion in combination with light.

Kenneth Martin avoids machines. He seeks for the fundamentals of movement and discovers that they are to be found everywhere, in man himself, in the variations of his moods, in the pulsation of the heart, in music. From studies in equilibrium he passed on to motion studies. He goes so far as to concentrate moments of motion in the motionless object, which consequently do not manifest in movement literally but potentially. He frames rhythms in space by means of simple little metal bars, which demand a slow and patient consideration and experimentation, a subtle sense of proportions and directions, and an imaginative faculty that is not focused on volume or outline but on the figure of the movement. There is nothing spectacular in this, but it is striking because of its purity and its concentration; 'One seeks to arrive at a single powerful image-object in which material, method, concept and feelings are indivisible.' As in Bernini's days, he experiments with water in the concept of a fountain (*Fountain in Stainless Steel,* 1961, Brixton Day College, London), in which the presence of the water has been used constructively as an element of motion. Up to the present, all his work has for its space a consciousness of form, in which the materials are not constituents, but nuclei charged with potential motion.

The date of the real reaction of the younger generation to the older one is approximately 1950. As after 1945 in Continental painting, the followers of the *Cobra* movement laid down the principle of vitality in opposition to the puritan austerity of abstraction culminating in Mondrian, so in England there came to the surface an urge towards greater freedom, towards relaxation, towards a less fundamental use of materials, in short, towards a relinquishing of the sacrosanct discipline in favour of imagination and expression. In painting, Sutherland and Francis Bacon drew the attention of a greater public.

Taboos, like those concerning eroticism, which had been eliminated earlier by D.H. Lawrence in literature, were now eliminated in the ruling insular aesthetics of art as an after-effect of surrealism.

The years between 1913 and 1917 were ill-disposed towards humanity, but kindly disposed towards sculpture: they saw the births of Butler (1913), Chadwick (1914), Meadows (1915), Armitage (1916), and Adams (1917). Then one has to wait about ten years for the birth of a second wave of future talents: Turnbull (1922), Dalwood (1924) and Paolozzi (1924).

As has been mentioned, they successively caught the attention of the public around 1950, at which time the art trade also started to occupy itself with them seriously.

In the vortex period, the Leicester Galleries ventured into the domain of pioneer sculpture (by Gaudier and others). In about 1950 the Gimpel Fils Gallery opened its doors to a number of younger sculptors.

The Fine Art Department of the British Council under the management of Mrs Lilian Somerville contributes not a little to an impressive representation of older and younger English sculptors abroad. Characteristic of the growing social acceptance of English sculpture is the increasing number of smaller and larger galleries that have included this sculpture in their programmes, (for instance the Waddington Galleries, the Hanover Gallery, Marlborough New London Gallery and the Rowan Gallery.)

Reg Butler, who in the war, as a conscientious objector, was allowed to work for a village smith and learned the art of forging, after he had given up his training and career as an architect, may be said to mark the change of direction after Moore and Barbara Hepworth. This is in no slight degree attributable to the fact that in 1954 an international jury awarded his maquette the grand prix in a contest for a *Monument to the Unknown Political Prisoner.* Although, disgracefully enough, it has never

EDUARDO PAOLOZZI
St Sebastian III, 1958-59

been executed up till now, it gave wide publicity to an English conception of open iron sculpture, the 'direct carving' idea being abandoned in favour of wrought iron. This process also has its old rural tradition. In Spain a Chillida is unimaginable without the old technique of the rustic smiths. On the occasion of his first exhibition in 1949, Butler introduced this fundamentally different view of the material, upon which he imposed the creative will of the form-determining artist. The figuration dating from 1948 is principally vertical with characteristic Gonzales-like details from the thirties, but towards 1951 these diminished considerably. His motive in 1951 was a 'reclining woman' a motive of Epstein's and later of Moore's. With the already loosening hold on it by Gonzales and Picasso, Butler turned it into a balanced figure.

The *Monument to the Unknown Political Prisoner* is severe and linear with a figuration that is modernized traditional in the unelaborated figures of the model. In fact the whole conception is ambivalent. It attacks on two fronts. The clever and dangerous trait in Butler is his rendering it

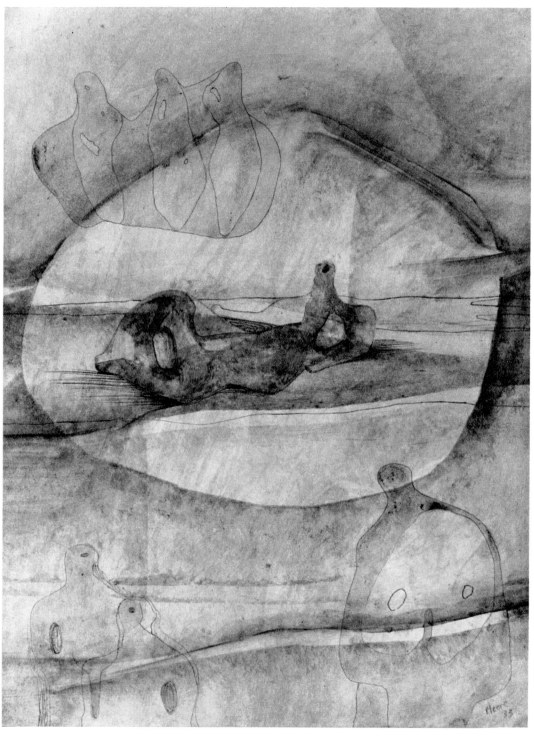

HENRY MOORE - *Drawing for sculpture*, 1933

acceptable. His further development is—quite obviously considering this attitude—fitful. The acrobatics of the female nudes, linked to linear constructions, are extremely ingeniously balanced, keenly observed, and highly suggestive of motion. The physical presence of these bronze figures (based once again on the modelling process) stands in a comprehensible relation to the nineteenth century and more particularly to Degas, whose studies of flying circus figures do not essentially deviate from Butler's. The vertical motive of the girls taking off their clothes was a reaction to the former more horizontal period of insects and reclining figures, but it was also a reaction to the open style and the contour. A sensitivity to rugged material and closed masses had set in so that, involuntarily, an affiliation to Medardo Rosso makes itself felt in the glorious rising of the form from the congealed lava of the bronze that had retained something of the glaze of the fire. It is to be expected that Butler's inner discord will suggest other motives to him, caught between an abstraction that at once attracts and repels him, and a figuration which seems inescapable as an (erotic) obsession, and which is constantly urging him from an open to a closed style. The 'towers' and 'watchers' have come into being with architectonic elements in the building up of still partly closed forms with a human essence. They cannot be called abstract. The structural force in them is identical with that which strikes us in the nudes, which are an amalgamation of architectonic sentiment and plastic power.

Patrick Heron has written that Butler is the 'Kafka of modern sculpture'. Such things are more easily written than proved. Fear, often also mentioned in the case of Chadwick (by Herbert Read), has never been constructive. (Germaine Richier was the only one in sculpture who was able to give form to the contradiction which is present in the form-impairing character of real essential fear.) The symbol of the open structure of the cage in which the closed human figure is held a prisoner is a balanced, perfectly controlled composition in which the ambivalence is made acceptable. The disquiet, the inner discord which is the consequence of this is wholly different from the fatal character of Kafka's destroying anxiety.

It is not astonishing that the name of Kafka is mentioned in connection with the host of insect-like beings, haunting animals, mythical combinations of human beings and animals which, shortly after Butler, became almost a characteristic of the English School. Comparisons with Kafka and Bacon's painting are too easily applied. Blossoming out in the literary field, they are fascinating, but very soon lose their relationship with the life of forms. In the same way the theory of 'dehumanization' developed by the Spanish philosopher Ortega y Gasset on literary-philosophical grounds has now entered art criticism and has, regrettably, proved to be far too fertile. The creation of a new object, a form charged with an energy all its own, is something that is hardly realized any longer. Just as Nicholson played an important part in the struggle of abstraction against surrealism, Graham Sutherland now uses insect forms in his paintings and aggressive motives. But is doubtful whether in this case one should speak of a strictly defined influence; perhaps the expression 'psychical climate' would be more accurate. It is only with a few artists that the animal and particularly the entomological style has the accent of the demoniacal, the subconscious, the terrified averting of a menace.

The medieval monastic world gave rise, in the miniatures and in the sculpture of the cathedrals, to fabled animals, monsters and chimeras, to a whole fauna which, in the beginning, showed the tensions of forces escaping from the oppression of the monastic rules, or which belonged to the apocalyptic imagination of a declining world. Later it is nothing but the interest in God's nature which forms the foundation of the aesthetics of the scenery.

The contemporary world is different. The collective terror (war and destruction), the collective reactive struggle against the heavy burden of a mechanized community also calls up individual reactions, and influences the creative impulses.

It would be possible to draw up an English iconography of the animal in present-day art, but it is, to a higher degree than it used to be, the image of the individually constructed animal, created by the artist as an apparition of his own emotional imaginative life.

Chadwick's animal is his very own property. It belongs neither to Otto Müller, nor to Raoul d'Haese, nor to Couzijn, nor to César. In Chadwick's work we are confronted with a creation that has a perfectly individual history. He has not enjoyed, like most artists in England, the training of one of the local or university art schools, or of the Royal College of Art. He worked in architects' offices, and in the war he was a pilot. When he was back in civil society as designer of textiles and an interior decorator, he started constructing mobiles, and later, balanced sculptures (*The Inner Eye* had a moving crystal); then the closed stabiles in series of animal motives, bird motives, human figures, dancers, strangers and watchers. His conception of architecture and interior decoration is still visible in the manner in which he reconstructed his own interior in a neo-Gothic country-house in Lypiatt Park near Stroud with an inventiveness which is a perfect union of his sense of space and his sense of sculpture, from which emerges furniture (tables, seats) deviating from every convention and perfectly embodied in the given space.

Thus, technically Chadwick tries to find what he thinks necessary to make a unit of matter and form. He uses rectilinear frameworks, which remain visible and are filled up with a kind of artificial stone, a mixture of plaster and iron. The structure is at the same time the visual rhythm, and through a special surface treatment the geometrical planes acquire the meaning of a skin. In a certain sense this schematization of the figure reminds one of the well-known sketches by the medieval architect Villard d'Honnecourt. But he started from the figure itself, he sought the mathematical quality of the human body, and in fact this was the architectonic element that became perceptible in the body.

Chadwick is living in a different time, but still the working process clearly shows a similarity to that used by Juan Gris in the cubist period. Gris has always stressed the fact that he started from 'the abstract side', which he humanized. Chadwick speaks of vitalizing abstraction. Gris says: 'I make a bottle—a particular bottle out of a cylinder. Hence, I never know in advance the appearance of the object represented.' He worked deductively. 'I start with an abstraction in order to arrive at a true fact' (Kahnweiler on Juan Gris, London, 1947). Chadwick, as Alan Bowness observes, 'starts with the abstract form and works towards the animal or figure'. The contrast with Gris and his time is to be found in a palpable participation of a subtle intelligence and an excessive consciousness in Gris, as opposed to a less inhibited influence of the subconscious, a weakened urge towards a representational object and a powerful, emotional, complex content, charged with psychical values in Chadwick.

The sculpture, brought about with greater accuracy, transmits something to the spectator, something which has a certain affinity with the conception of an animal or a bird; yet it is not the animal or bird from nature, but the 'Chadwick animal', the 'Chadwick bird' or the 'Chadwick stranger'.

Chadwick took sculpture back to a standstill, a standing fixed in space, which gives the immobility the value of being able to explode at any moment, to jump away—an expectation, a listening for, as in the case of a loaded gun, the trigger to be drawn. The accuracy of the forms constructed from rectilinear frame-works and little planes intensifies the sensation of a dangerous presence. Chadwick has created concrete realities, mythical animals emanating from his own vital reality. Obviously he himself is

36

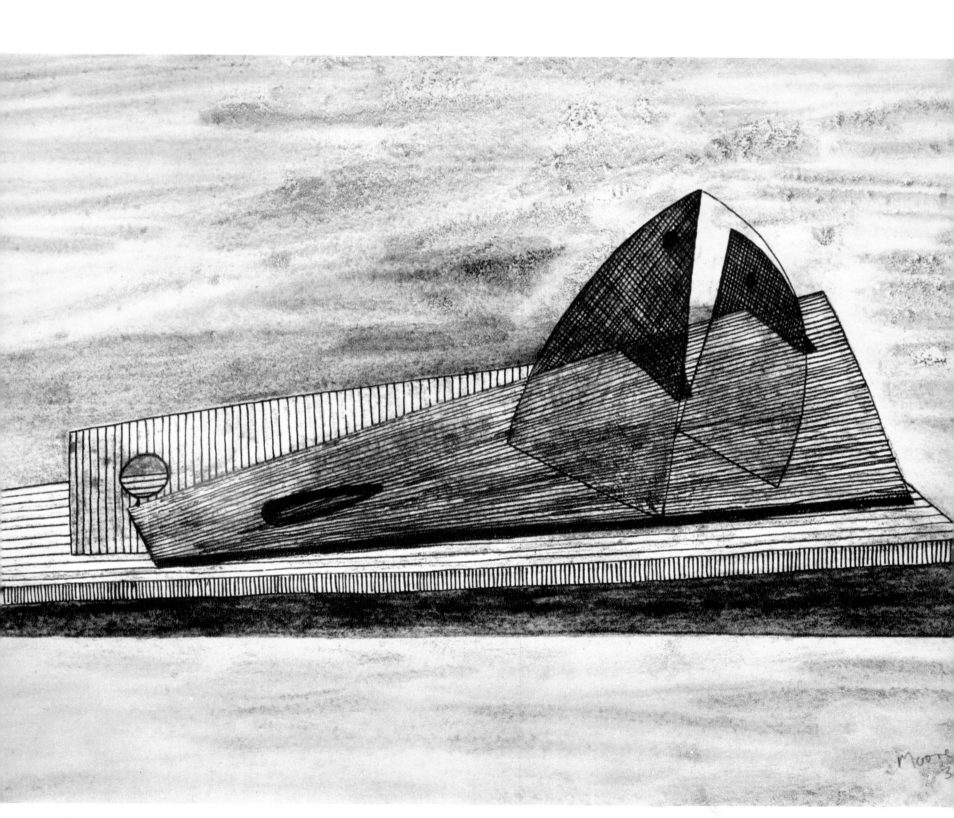

HENRY MOORE - *Drawing for Sculpture (wood construction)*, 1933

37

dominated by a motive that, once it has come into being, reacts on him and gives birth to the same motive, though altered, drawing from the source of energy by which a motive can again and again set in motion creative activity. When the energy, with which a motive is constructively charged, is exhausted, a new process begins for the formation of a new motive. Chadwick exercised an influence. He gave rise to an unscholastic ('unschoolish') sculpture that is based on a particularly pure, genuine world of sensations. Without his foundation of an architectonic practice this would probably have ended in a more capricious and more surrealistic expression. For it is not the mental control and the intellectual creation of order that strike us in his constructions, but a kind of armistice between the inner and outer being, between emotional vision and matter, between motion and immobility.

Among those who contributed a part in the development of animal sculpture, Bernard Meadows principally occupies himself with the aggressiveness of birds and with crustacea. He was one of Henry Moore's assistants before the war (from 1936 to 1939).

Though some critics mention Chadwick as an influence, his technique and especially his tense, powerful form have nothing to do with Meadows' creations. Essentially Meadows makes a much more pictorial sculpture, which is reminiscent of Sutherland. In his more recent work we are struck by the *Seated Armed Figure* (1962) in which something of Armitage may be perceived—an analogous way of limiting the legs to a simple indication—but with heavier accents in the volume.

Kenneth Armitage did not spare himself in his development. Originally fascinated by Egypt and being a clever sculptor of the direct-carving principle, he later not only rejected this tradition, but also destroyed his work. As since that time he has been working in plaster, bronze has become his medium. In his motives there predominates, in contrast to Chadwick, the fluctuating, mobile element.

It is quite a curious sensation to hear his own statement about bronze, from which one sees that not only is there a technical deviation from the Moore-Hepworth road, but that the climate has undergone a psychical alteration too. 'I work rather impatiently with ideas or images, and prefer a medium that helps me easily and quickly to get what I want. I have always been interested in bronze casting, mainly for the fluid, unifying and sensual quality it can give.' Here the artist's impatience is speaking, the swiftness and directness of the impulses.

Just like Chadwick he fears a surplus of conscious control as well as a disturbing of the original source and its outlet, within which the preparatory formation of the motives occurs. In ponderous writings critics have commented upon the plastic combination of two or more figures, which Moore did once in a while and then only briefly, which led Chadwick with much wit and subtle mockery to fascinating inventions, and which Armitage does with his developed consciousness of the relief in works which are often lyrical, but for which he was also able to find monumental solutions (*Triarchy,* 1958-59). The art critic James Fitz Simmons (*Quadrum* No 6; 'Space and the Image in Art') sees in it 'the human life at the bovine level' and goes so far as to see the coupled figures as symbolic reductions, which become an incestuous horror figuration. This reasoning, based on an interpretation of the motive, can only be corrected if one forms a clear idea of the remarkable accents which Armitage applies to the skin of the volume. These accents are extremely concise indications of form that presuppose an intense observation and the interpretation of life seen (in its full meaning) by an ardent, deep and poetic artist. He wants a large form or surface in order to let emerge from it the tokens (not the details) by which he makes his vision known. And this vision is teeming with sensual and witty, ironical elements.

Armitage has a sense of humour, a feeling for the light touch, for play-

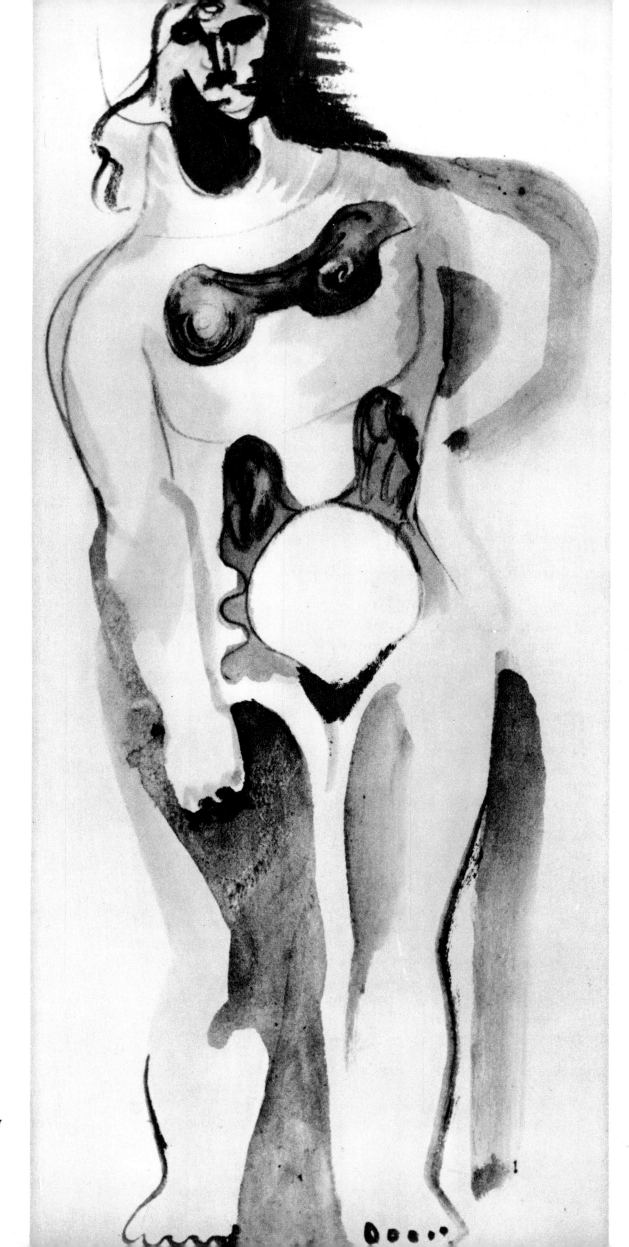

HENRY MOORE
Life Drawing - Standing Woman, 1927

fulness, which has always been rare in sculpture and in fact was only possible when a somewhat baroque modelling admitted the creation of the capricious. It is easy to see the danger of this (a naturalism among other things), but it should never make us blind to the struggle which Armitage has had in order to realize in an adequate form his own particular vision of men and groups—a realization with a surrealistic poetic inclination.

Robert Adams is an exception in the generation of Chadwick, Armitage and Meadows. He prefers working in steel, but also uses wood. This means that his feeling for the hard metal may join in the expression of the form, which is rectangular, circular or tube-shaped (in exceptional cases fluid as in *Growing Forms* 1954, Sycamore), but is drawn towards the human character by the nature of the material. With Adams abstraction always acquires mobility, the severity of the planes is invariably mitigated by the presence of a sensitive spot, where something else is happening, where a perforation takes place, or a different rhythm of the small planes or a change in the direction. His half-open screens (1962) have an almost Mondrian-like atmosphere, a provoking rhythm of little triangles. The coat of silver or bronze on the surface has an aesthetic and protective function. The best modern theatre to date, built in Gelsenkirchen (Western Germany) shows that the authorities understood what Robert Adams signified in regard to a severely stylized architecture. The 72 ft long and 9 ft high relief, executed in ferro-concrete, proudly shows a great style.

With Oliffe Richmond, we come to another one-time assistant of Moore who also discovered Rodin in a certain dramatic character of massive figures, bearers of burdens, dark in nature, heavy of tread with the accent (as in Armitage) less on the legs than on the whole bulk of the body, but (unlike Armitage) the head fluently included in the expressiveness of the figure.

Ralph Brown (Richmond's junior by nine years) while never one of Moore's assistants, appears in his youthful work very much under the spell of Moore's personality, but curiously enough more under that of the earlier than of the later Moore. As he freed himself from this influence, he showed in his more recent work (1960-63) an as yet unquiet development. The typically English theme 'King and Queen' started by Moore and taken up again by Armitage, acquires in Brown's *Queen* an erotically animal or even magical symbolism. It would be possible to write an essay on the theme furnished by the rulers of England. In *Minotaure* No 9, 1936, Edward James wrote an excellent study on 'Le Chapeau du peuple et les chapeaux de la Reine' (The hat of the people and the hats of the Queen—then Queen Mary). The surrealistic deformation, presumably also evoked by Bacon's paintings, that shows itself in Brown's sculptures, demonstrates certain changes in the anachronistic royalist feelings that were still deeply rooted in 1936.

Armitage also influences Brown, but not his lightness, playfulness, warmth. Among the youngest generation Elisabeth Frink (1930) is still clinging to Meadows' and Armitage's bird motives; she shows figures which, as silhouettes, but particularly because of the gestures, produce a powerful effect, and show a delicate plastic gradation in the totality of the mass. In a recent figuration, *The Dead King* (1962-63) the royal motive once more occupies her too, but it is more personal of vision and freer from influences.

The trio Turnbull, Dalwood and Paolozzi dissociated themselves from Butler, Chadwick and Armitage. Dalwood took lessons with Armitage in Bath. His work does not show any affinity with this training any more. When one thinks of the importance Chadwick attaches to the surface, of Armitage's play with accents in a plane, one is forced to the conclusion that Hubert Dalwood still belongs to those who inscribe the surface with a writing, which we might read as the relief symbols on the Sumerian

HENRY MOORE
Studies for Reclining Figure, 1937

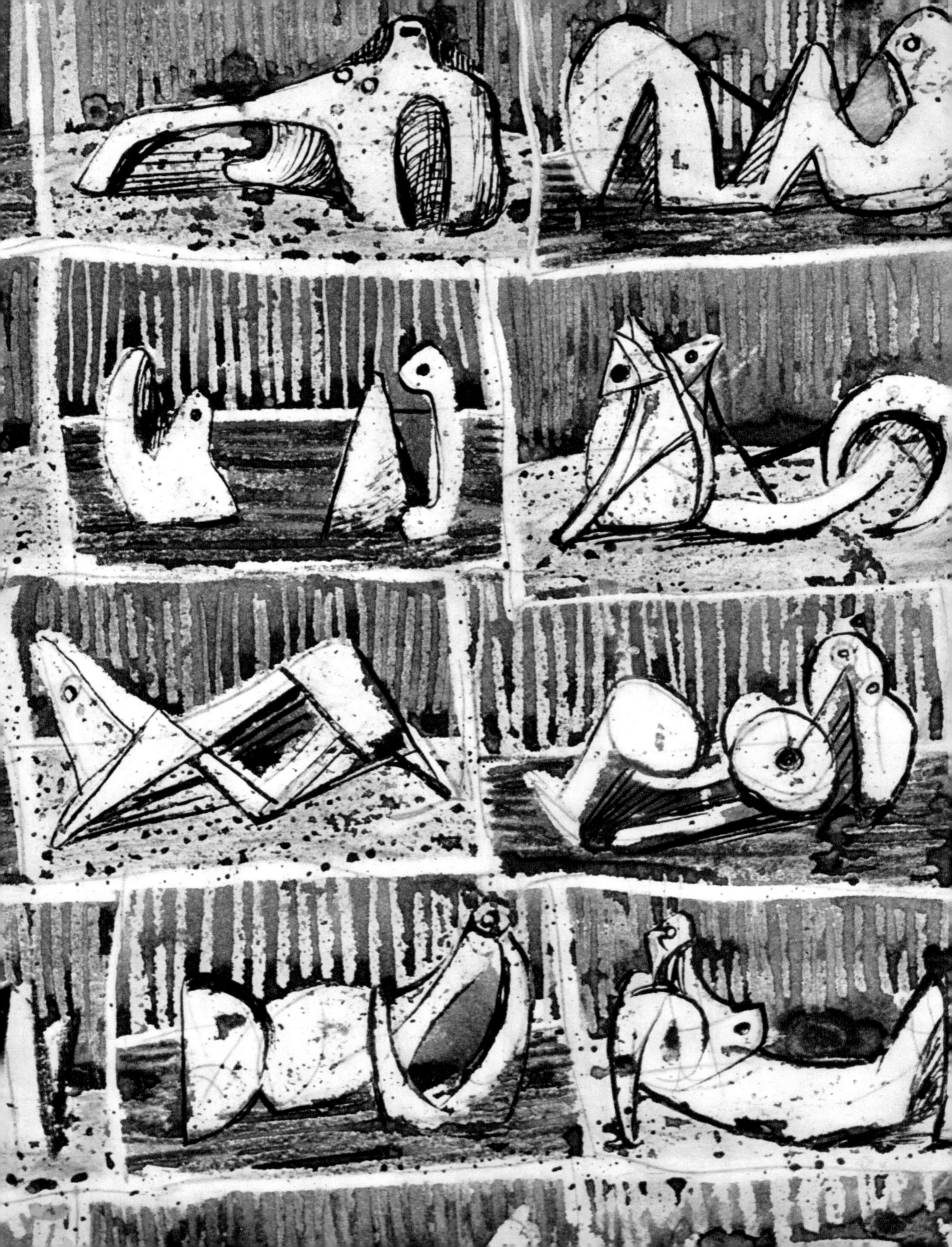

and Accadian seal rolls. However, Dalwood also works in spatial forms, but always from a moulded smaller model in bronze.

After a period spent as a designer for the Bristol Aeroplane Company, his initial activities were, as late as 1956, directed towards the compact human figure. After this we see the birth of free forms of imagination, which have something of the archaic and ritual character of old Chinese bronzes. His titles *Soldier, Orb, Minos, Queen* (a Queen again!), *High Judge,* demand of the spectator that he frees himself from the visual, conventional image they evoke. For Dalwood makes singular objects which have no psychical relationship with their titles, and which are neither a recognizable symbol nor an abstraction. They are beautifully built up, well-proportioned, not derived from nature but from human objects. They are things born of things, and turned into new appearances, as illegible and as fascinating as Babylonian writing (in relief or in space).

It is purely plastic, without gambling on effects that are foreign to plastic art and at the same time full of a quality which I believe is identical with the miracle by which man can create. And this is what Dalwood does, directly, convincingly, without melodrama. If he retains this talent, his importance will undoubtedly penetrate more deeply.

William Turnbull, painter and sculptor, began (cf. Paolozzi) by digesting an influence of Giacometti, which immediately reveals his surrealistic sensitivity. In 1949 he occupied himself with mobiles. As a painter he knew what the Americans were doing (Kline, Rothko, and Pollock). Coupled with his interest in prehistoric idols, his background is therefore complicated, but clearly directed and coherent.

As a sculptor he thinks in spheres, columns, cylinders, but as in the case of Dalwood, the treatment of the skin of the material means much to him, so that the typically geometrical and abstract elements of the basic forms get blurred. The basic forms become idols. One can read runes on them that are his individual writing. He denies that his graphic hatchings are treatments of the surface. 'I used texture to invoke chance, to create random discoveries, not to elaborate the surface, but to accentuate that it was a skin of bronze.' Nevertheless these elaborations of the material remain confined to the periphery but the intention is no longer aesthetic. With striking instinctive penetration he makes precise comments: 'The skin is that fragile boundary between our inside and outside space—and the eye sees the most fragile connection between the two areas. What a tremendous decision to destroy this. That is my fascination with the Indians, who blinded themselves by looking at the sun, or the self-blinding Oedipus.' Out of this world of feelings, equilibrium sculptures are born, such as *The Sungazer* (1959). Another amazement gives rise to a series of loose heads painted and sculptured. 'The word "head" meant for me what I imagined the word "landscape" had meant for some painters—a format that could carry different loadings.' In this way, a motive formed in his mind, indicated by the nonfixed meaning of 'head'. But the motive itself comes into existence through the wish to be free from the wearing out of words, and to try to penetrate the moment of the first stammered appellation. This same ability to be free from the common usage and the conventions explains his attitude towards matter. He wants to escape from bronze as a dominant, and seeks a combination of wood, stone and bronze. As far as observing and creating is concerned, his attitude towards nature is no longer tied to the forms of nature. He experiences his own creative energy and action as an activity parallel to nature.

Finally there is Eduardo Paolozzi, whose Italian origin, notwithstanding his youth and training in Edinburgh, remains perceptible. Owing to the nature of his work and his influence he has been looked upon as a man who breaks through the English headquarters of sculpture, who no longer has any relationship with the Moore-Hepworth period, but who found his sources in the early dadaists and surrealists in Paris, particularly in

HENRY MOORE - *Drawing for sculpture: Ideas for Stringed Figures, 1938*

Tristan Tzara, in the poetically intellectual centre, and further in Picasso, Giacometti and Brancusi. 'Dada Surrealism' was also a movement in England before the second World War. One has only to think of Roland Penrose, Paul Nash, Mesens and others, but Paolozzi (in a conversation with Roditi) states as his opinion that in reality the English understood it as 'humour'. To him it means an attitude to life, and not a means of getting excitement via nonsense. With him the poetry of the absurd becomes a value in sculpture.

Paolozzi, who worked in Paris from 1947-49, came back to England with continental inventions, and out of assorted parts of machines (cog-wheels, letters, disks) he created his heads (which, unlike Turnbull's, had necks) and figures, after a period of incessant experimenting lasting nearly five years. As Gaudier had done in the Vortex period, but at that time in a vacuum, Paolozzi introduced elements of the *Ecole de Paris* into London again, where they proved to be fruitful. In his case this meant at first a state of isolation in the midst of English sculpture which had very different tendencies. Now there are sympathizers enough. Until recently Paolozzi was a man of detail, even a man obsessed by detail. His figures get absorbed in an open space as totalities and also as contours. They are more a 'presence' than an appearance, and as a definition of 'presence' the word 'magic' is often used.

Let it be said here that to use the word 'magic' and also 'cosmic' too freely is not advisable. At best we can speak in our society of a faint whiff of magic if an artist has an affinity with archaic forms or times, and his work is able to transmit something of it to the spectator. The old animistic belief that the sculptor in creating his work gives life to a beneficial or evil power, has lost its force. Aesthetic intentions already make a mess of the magic use of sculpture.

Perhaps we may speak, but then in a negative sense, of magic emotions in the public (only remember the reactions in London to Epstein's sculptures), if in matters of sculpture the taboo is aggressively applied by mutilating the images or having them removed under the hypocritical pretext of their immorality.

It is clear that Paolozzi in the first place literarily but also visually, assimilated the world of dada and surrealism, and that his mental disposition is in accordance with this in the things of today. But it is no less true that the revolutionary and anarchist impulses in the old movements are now lacking, as they are lacking in pop—and junk-art. The resumption of what happened in Zürich in the first World War, and after that in Paris and New York, found in the years between 1950 and 1964 an altered society and a different response. Paolozzi and his group are not 'anti-art', nor are they 'anti-museums'. Paolozzi even likes museums, and the fact that he is making art does not disturb him.

In contrast with the intentional neglect of the durability of the 'collages' and other products, Paolozzi exerts himself technically to render his combinations as durable as possible. This too is the result of the changed surrealist attitude.

'L'objet trouvé' is cast 'à cire perdu' via negatives impressed in clay. He does not use his material in the rough, but constructs his figures out of these pieces. Thus, the riot of the surrealist years meets the tradition of the work of art of the much abused bourgeois society, and the two enter into matrimony. The result is that the anti-craftsmanship theory cedes ground. It became obvious that the aversion was only directed against a special kind of craftsmanship. The *Forms on a Bow* is related to Giacometti's atmosphere in 1930-32; Paul Nash also has a somewhat similar sculpture (*The Archer*) reproduced in *Minotaure* No 8, 1936. In the large figures *His Majesty the Wheel* and the *Sebastian* series, the structure has lost its prominence, only to return in the austerely constructed, stable symmetrical sculptures, which are unexpected phenomena. Perhaps they should be looked upon as a reaction to his love of the exuberant detail, to the absence of structure, to the semi-transparency of the past, which now gets consolidated. In short, we find an apparent contradiction with the previous character of his sculpture. *Apparent,* for what remains is the surprising, the quasi-timeless quality of this nineteenth-century furniture, constructed out of parts of machines in a spirit which ironically uses the old monumentality: neo-classicism. In a certain sense it is also discarded things, picked up by Paolozzi, and created anew out of the agility, the abrupt unrest of his constantly amazed mind. In spite of all consolidation, all regressive invention, the ever watchful, universal amazement remains alive.

At present more young artists are working in this same atmosphere. Pop- and junk-art are attractive. Seen in the context of the whole English development they mean an active participation in and a being open to an international phenomenon, without as yet any development of leading qualities, as was the case in the period between the two wars. But it may still happen. There are sculptors of the same age as Dalwood and Paolozzi (born 1924) with fascinating talents: Fullard, Caro, Clarke and the slightly older John Hoskin (born 1921). The latter, who works with contrasts in the treatment of the surface of steel, has a clean, structurally convincing and powerful style.

Different from the metal-technique of Hoskin are the cast and forged iron works of Geoffrey Clarke (born 1924), who with his background of cooperation with architects and projects for stained glass and tapestry, likes to make sculptures with a modern symbolic primitive sense. He uses welded iron and has found a way of casting in aluminium and making the surface alive. The material is important to him. He belongs to the already elder generation which, unlike Caro and Fullard, follows the old way of pure form on the basis of the character of the material and symbolic feeling. More playful, more American is Fullard, who, with the use of existing fragments of furniture and doors, constructs ingenious figurations, which have, as in the case of the younger Morland (born 1934) a certain affinity with what Louise Nevelson has been doing in New York for years in a grander style. We follow with curiosity the surrealistic Phillip King, with simple, even elegant, forms and colours.

In the more than fifty years of English sculpture, those between 1930 and 1940 are of particular importance for the international and directive influence exerted by the works of Henry Moore and more especially, by reason of their abstract qualities, the works of Barbara Hepworth. This position, conquered in a laborious struggle, has added the authority of London, or rather of Great Britain, to that of Paris in the domain of plastic art.

Around 1950 it became evident that the younger artists broke through the limitation of what cannot be called essentially a 'school', inspired by a craving for liberty, which urged them to investigate what the old sources of dada-surrealism, but now rid of the obsolete 'anti' spirit and the predilection for noisy rows, still mean for the art of today. In this the motorial energy of surrealism is no longer active. Whether the magic element comes into play wholly depends on the genuine character of the force by which the reality of the things can be drawn into the inexpressible, and also on the reaction of the spectator. At any rate the postwar English surrealist sensitivity has confined itself to aesthetics, and by doing this has conjured up in sculpture a sphere of new sensations which may be said to join similar continental and American trends.

The period of purification is now the past. Qualities of clarity are no longer predominant. The new generation is playing with a few extra-sculptural elements, with an increasing will to surpass dada and surrealistic ambiances, leaving the shock-meaning aside, enlarging the field of motives and aesthetic awareness.

Though the iron sculptures have caused the development of typically English figures, such as insects, beasts and fabled human beings, the question remains what will be the way out of the stylistic derivations that subsequently have become visible.

There has come into being a formal and spiritual complexity in the phenomenon of the existence of an English sculpture, which half a century ago was something unthinkable.

The most recent development of English sculpture now proceeds from the generation that was born between 1930 and 1940. Though they do not constitute a group or a school their work shows certain similar characteristics. These are evident in their reactions (generally of a negative nature) to the whole of English twentieth-century sculpture including Epstein, Gaudier, Moore and Barbara Hepworth, and not only their immediate elders Butler, Chadwick, Armitage and Paolozzi—artists who are all still very active.

Those who expected—and personally I was one of them—that Paolozzi as the initiator of a new trend would become the leading influence on the younger artists—made a mistake. The leader, whose position may partly be explained by the fact that in practice he is also a teacher, is Anthony Caro. It was clear that Paolozzi led English sculpture from the Hepworth-Moore era back to a Parisian-dada-surrealist atmosphere, with more than a fair chance that the autonomous character of the English sculptors would fade away.

Anthony Caro, as a pupil of Moore's, showed his independence. With metal and colours in severe planes and lines, he attempted to discard the emotionally charged volume in favour of a restrained, objectively direct art, whose consequences are perhaps best shown by David Annesley (born 1936) with regard to directness, control and balance.

The group characteristic is an aversion to the figurative and abstract possibilities that are connected with the material of stone and bronze, which means an antipathy to direct carving—to doing things oneself—the renouncement of material resistances and of the ethics of honesty in face of the nature of the material. This means the suppression of an important part of sculpture. There is even a dissociation from the technical concept which, by means of drawings and indications, is left to specialists skilled in the use of such raw materials as plastics, plexiglass, polyester, aluminium, etc. It can be said that Rodin had his assistants, and that Gabo has to leave much to technicians. At present however the technical executant plays an increasingly important role. All that was abhorred by the progressive artists since the beginning of the twentieth century in regard to the character of the nineteenth century: the withdrawal from direct carving, the reliance on the skill of assistants, the weakening of contact with matter for the sake of a spurious fantasy, all this has changed as a result of this new attitude, or at least is no longer looked upon as important. Another phenomenon connected with this characteristic is the amalgamation of painting and sculpture. In nineteenth-century sculpture the pictorial element predominated. With the new predilection for painted surfaces and for paint in general, the colour is given a preponderance wholly different from the function of the colour which Zadkine and Picasso used in their early sculpture, and which was also used by Lipchitz, Archipenko, Arp, Barbara Hepworth and Vantongerloo. When Archipenko introduced the term 'sculpto-painting', shape and volume were still fundamental and the touch-point in painting was the *collage* and the *papier collé*. At present a 'non-associative colour sensation' is what they want to achieve with paint. At this point however question-marks are allowed. Ian Dunlop, who wrote the introduction to the Whitechapel catalogue of the exhibition 'The New Generation 1965' in which Bryan Robertson got

46

together a number of these young sculptors, is of the opinion in conformity with the views of the artists, that 'colour is perhaps the most obviously new thing about this sculpture' and 'the skin helps to rid sculpture of relying on tactile associations for its effects, and concentrates attention on its visual significance alone'. However, the paint, the colour-skin, that is used with these intentions most certainly calls up associations which are not emotional but—and this indeed is what is new about it—are to be found in the field of scent and taste. The choice of colour irresistibly evokes associations with sweets, soft drinks, perfumes, ice-creams, and so on. From a biologically psychical point of view these associations lead to a different domain; they are not spatial, but indispensable if the artist wants to create a certain mood in the spectator. Furthermore, the notion that the tactile sense should be suppressed is an illusion. Some of the visitors could not resist—according to my own prolonged observations —the temptation to try to discover the true nature of the materials by means of tapping. Of course the disappearance of the plinth is one of the elements conducive to an effect of weightlessness, but historically there is nothing new in it (Gabo, Arp, Calder, Marta Pan).

In my opinion a typical circumstance is the curious urge towards a new Byzantine attitude in regard to life, a revived vorticist aesthetic system. In the nineteenth century and the beginning of the twentieth century— in literature especially, but also in art—this culminated in the ideal of 'the dead face', the body bereaved of expression, the stilled, desire-less gesture, 'the rejected vitality'. It was the repression of the personal egocentric emotions, the disintegration of one's sensibility in regard to the exterior world, a withdrawal from matter, from organic life in favour of 'a higher truth of life'. It was not surrealism, but because of its transformation of the objects, aiming at an unsubstantial, aesthetically hybrid world, in part erotic, in part dreamily visionary and aloof, surrealism had a certain affinity with this world of the Japanese Nô-mask, the aesthetic byzantinism of a modern world.

In his deviation from the general trend Roland Piché (born 1938) is strongest. But what he positively demonstrates is the confusion of pictorial and sculptural qualities. He has a tension incompatible with 'the Doctrine', something of a mixture of Giacometti's dreams and the *terribilità* of Bacon's distortions and cages; a very personal dramatic approach full of qualities. The other one who is, in contrast with Piché, a partaker in the withdrawal from the emotional elements from the past, is Phillip King (born 1934). He has a particularly attractive, sometimes elegant, formal way to evoke new surrealistic tunes in space, to create, with the inside and the outside of simple geometrical forms, a world full of associations which he stimulates with not unimportant titles like: *And the Birds began to Sing* or *Ghengis Khan*. He underlines the poetical vision. King has a style of his own, and—which is important—the style of imagination.

'On the margin' of the past and the present seems to be Isaac Witkin (born 1936). His materials—wood, fibre glass—are not indifferent to him. His forms have associations with some organic vitality. There is a metamorphosis in his work, powerful and attractive.

The limitations of this trend, which does not form a group, but whose adherents have analogous aims, are obvious. As a result of the suppression of the materials and the dependence on a special kind of colour the possibilities are soon exhausted in the region of a passive, disembodied dreaming away of life according to the rules of the divorce *a mensa et thoro* from sculpture. Apart from vitality and action new dreams have been evoked, new experiments attempted.

THE PLATES

The captions for the following plates are to be found on pages 161 - 163

51

54

56

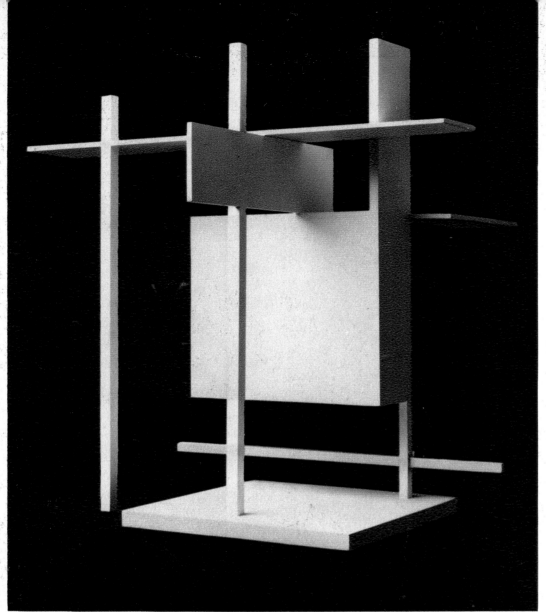

64

65

67

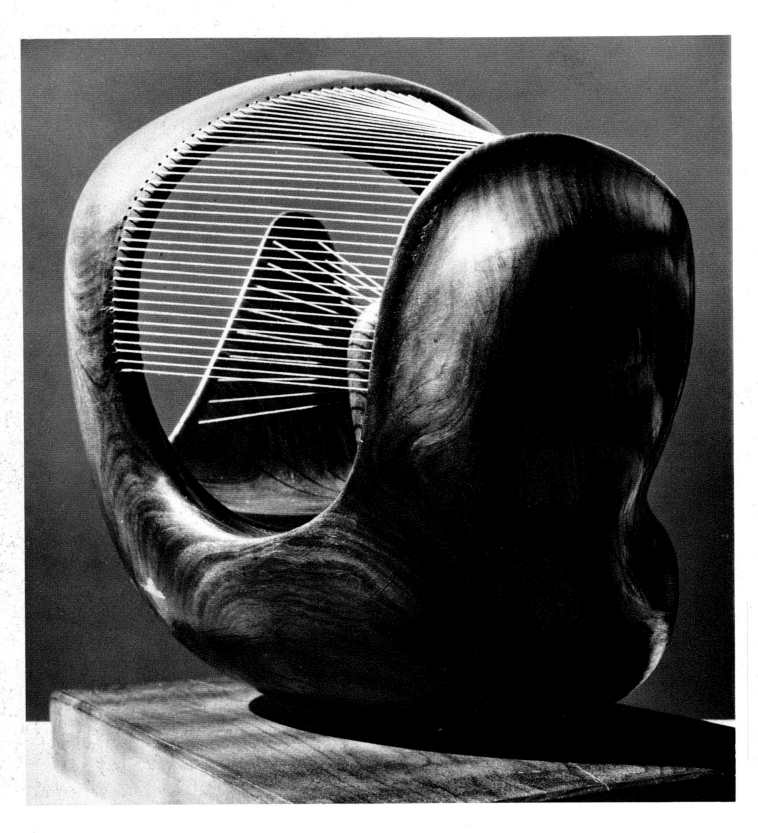

71

72

81

83

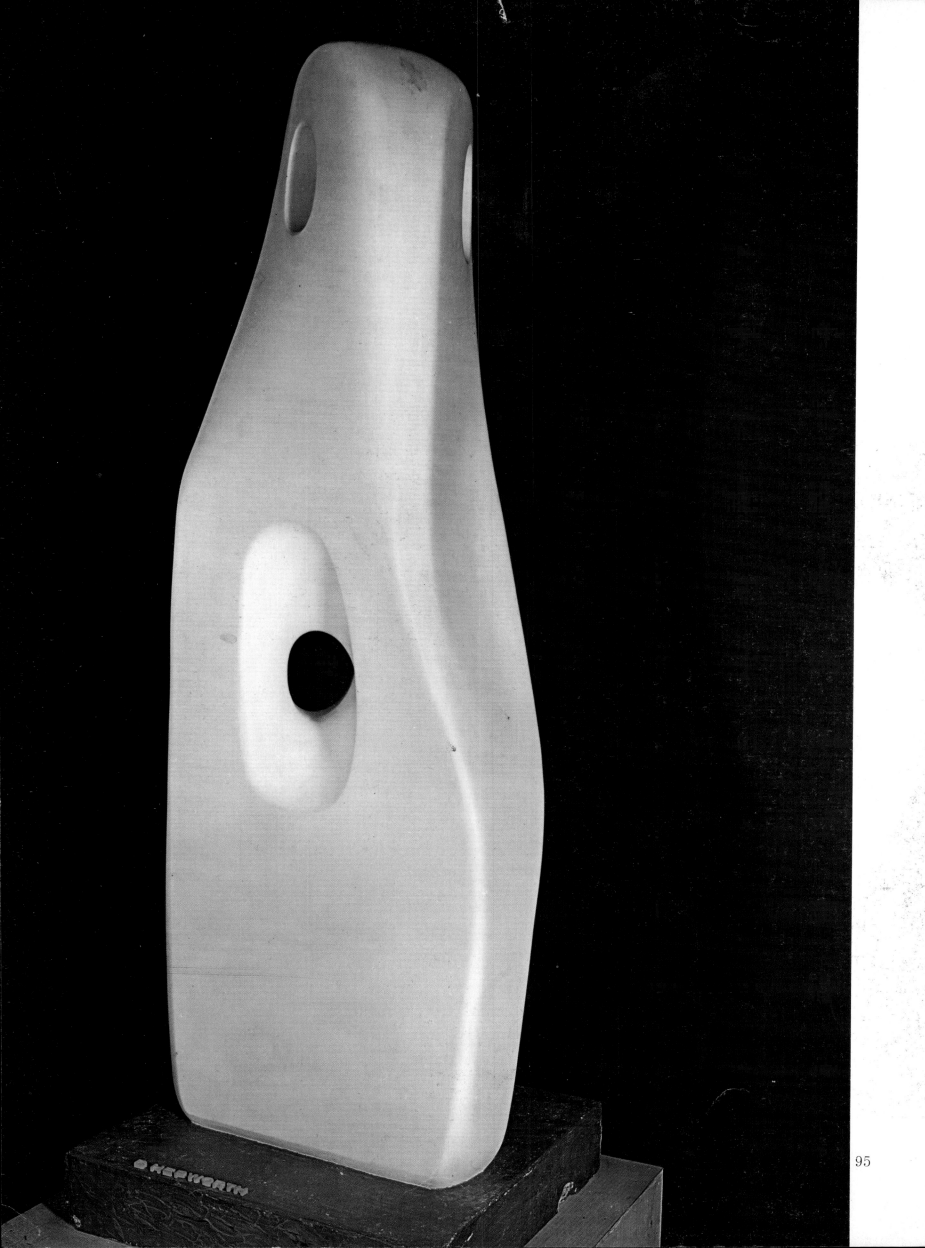

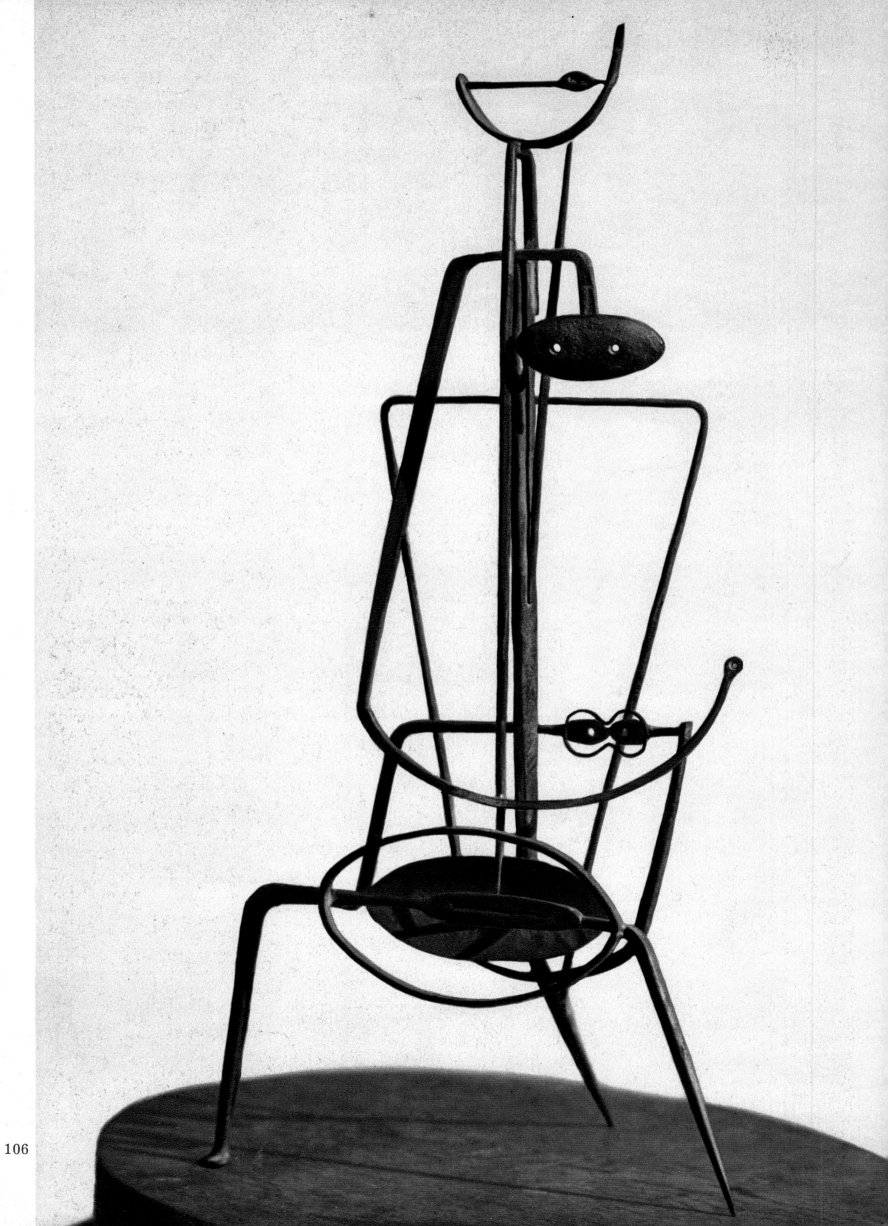

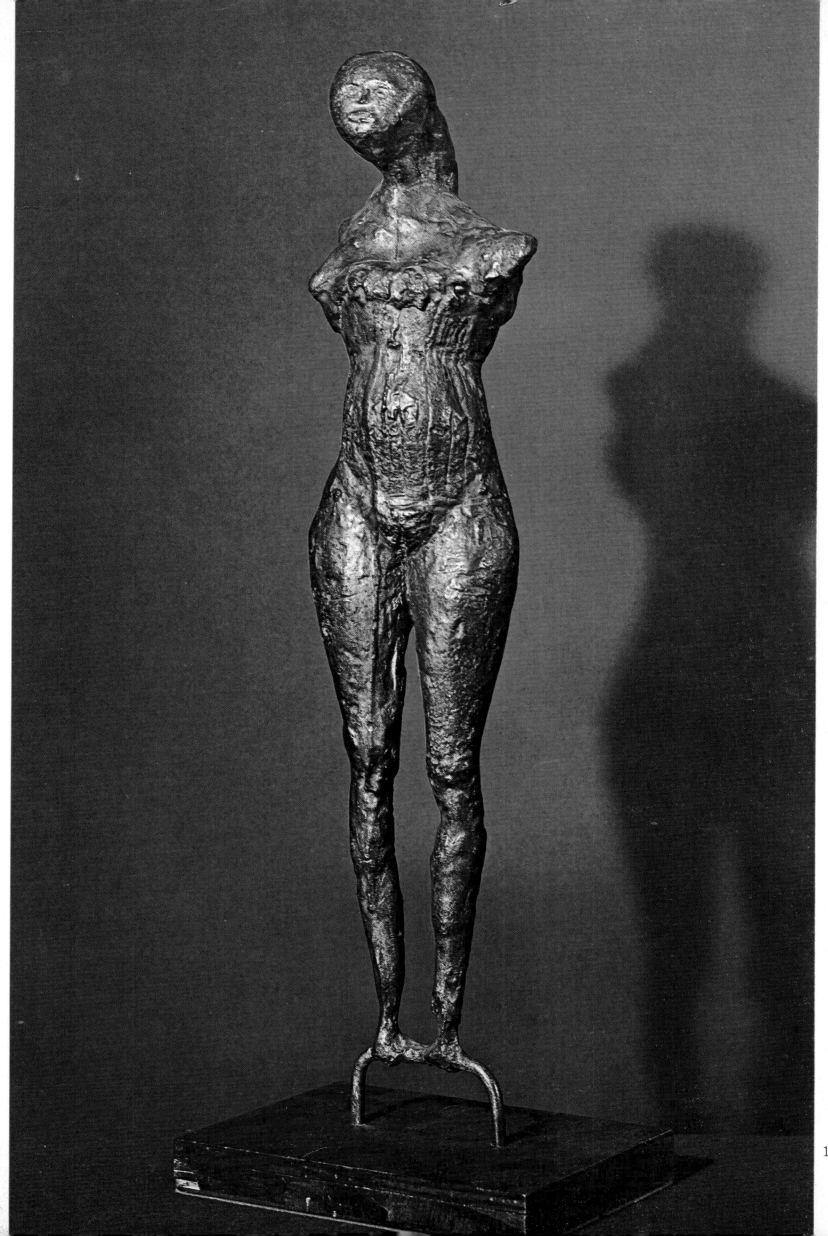

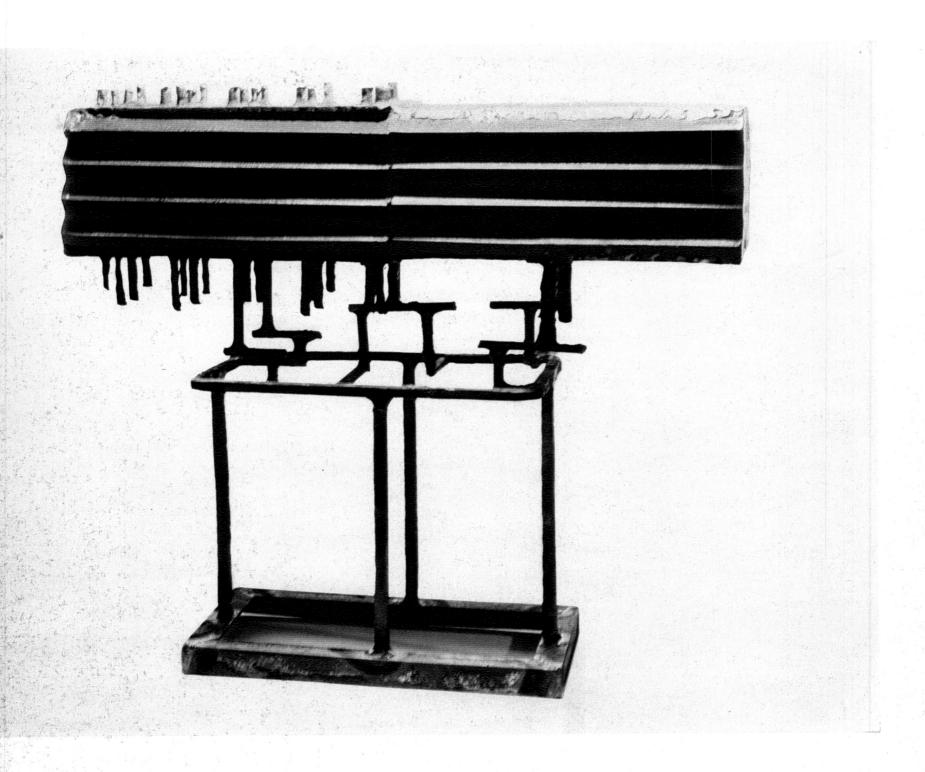

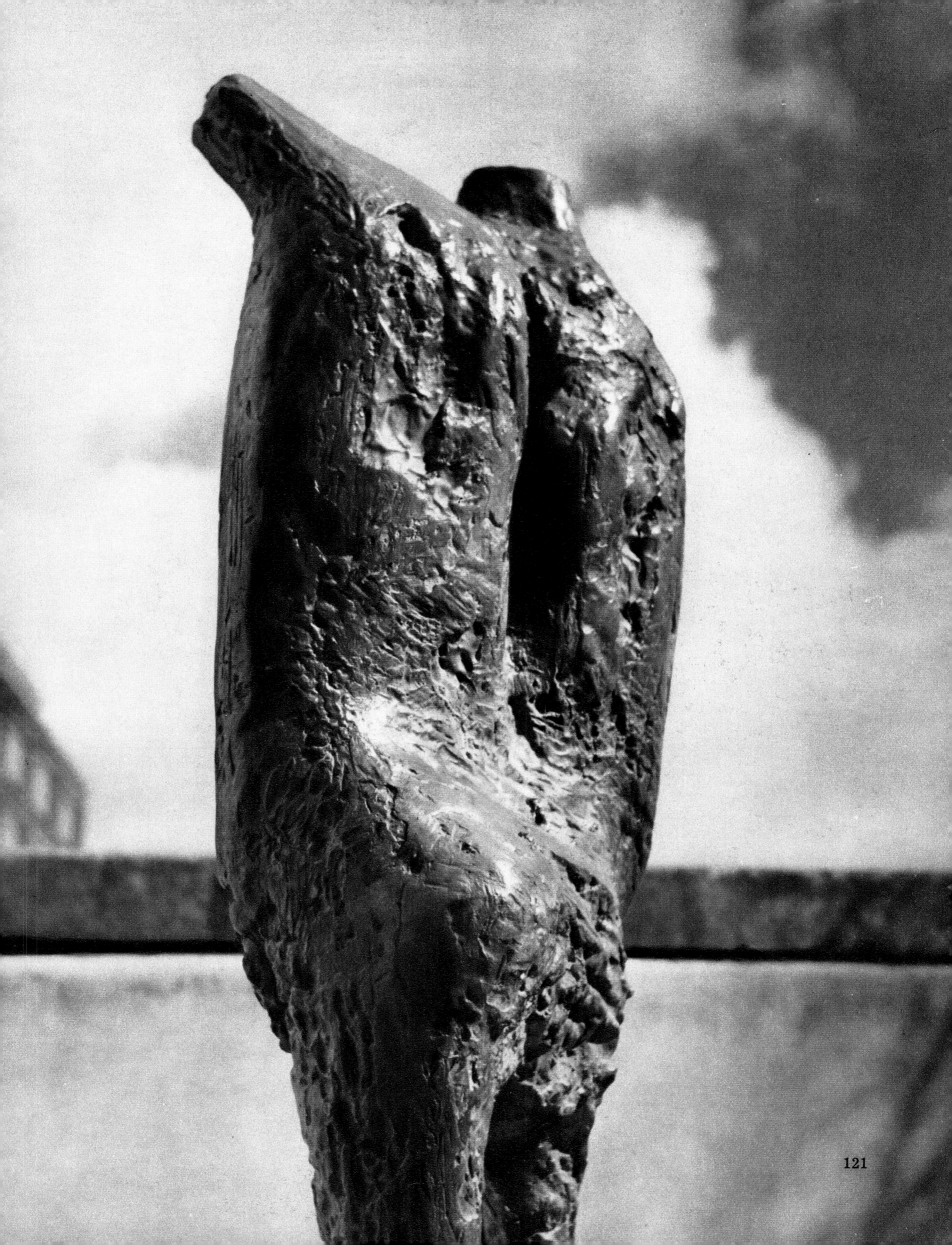

121

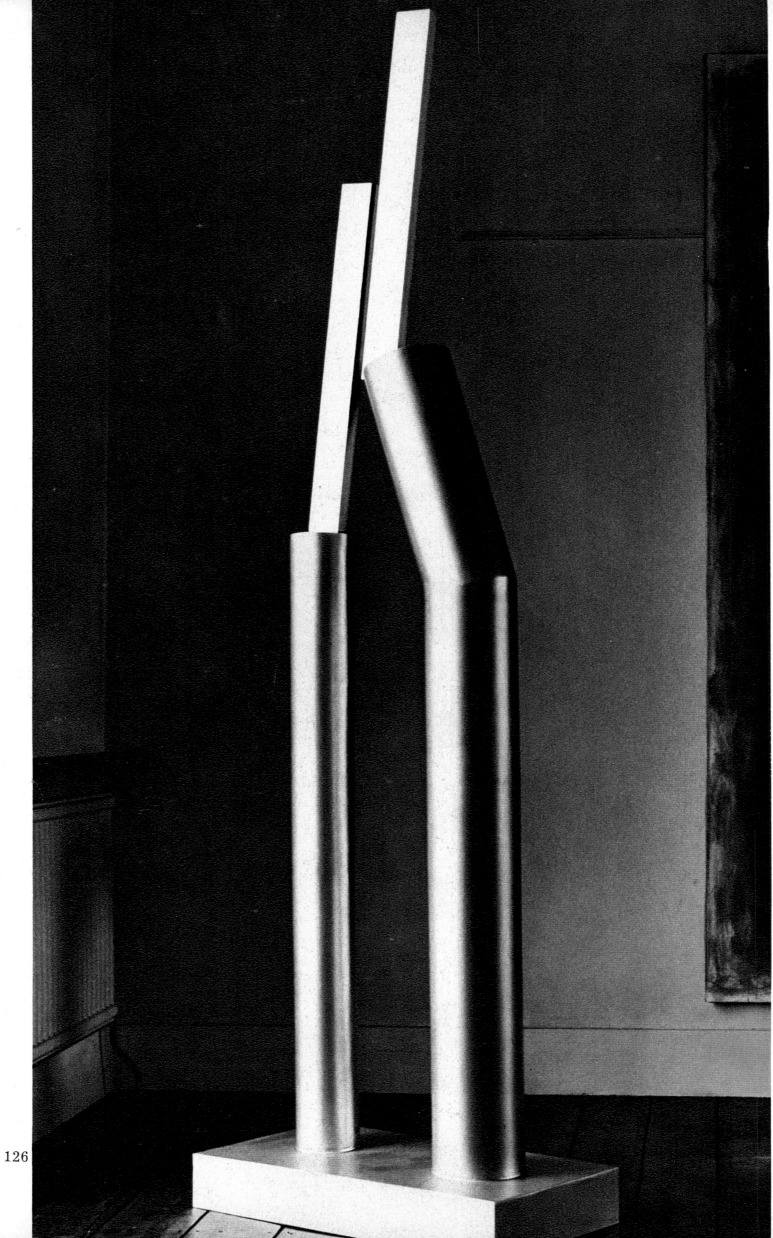

134

135

136

137

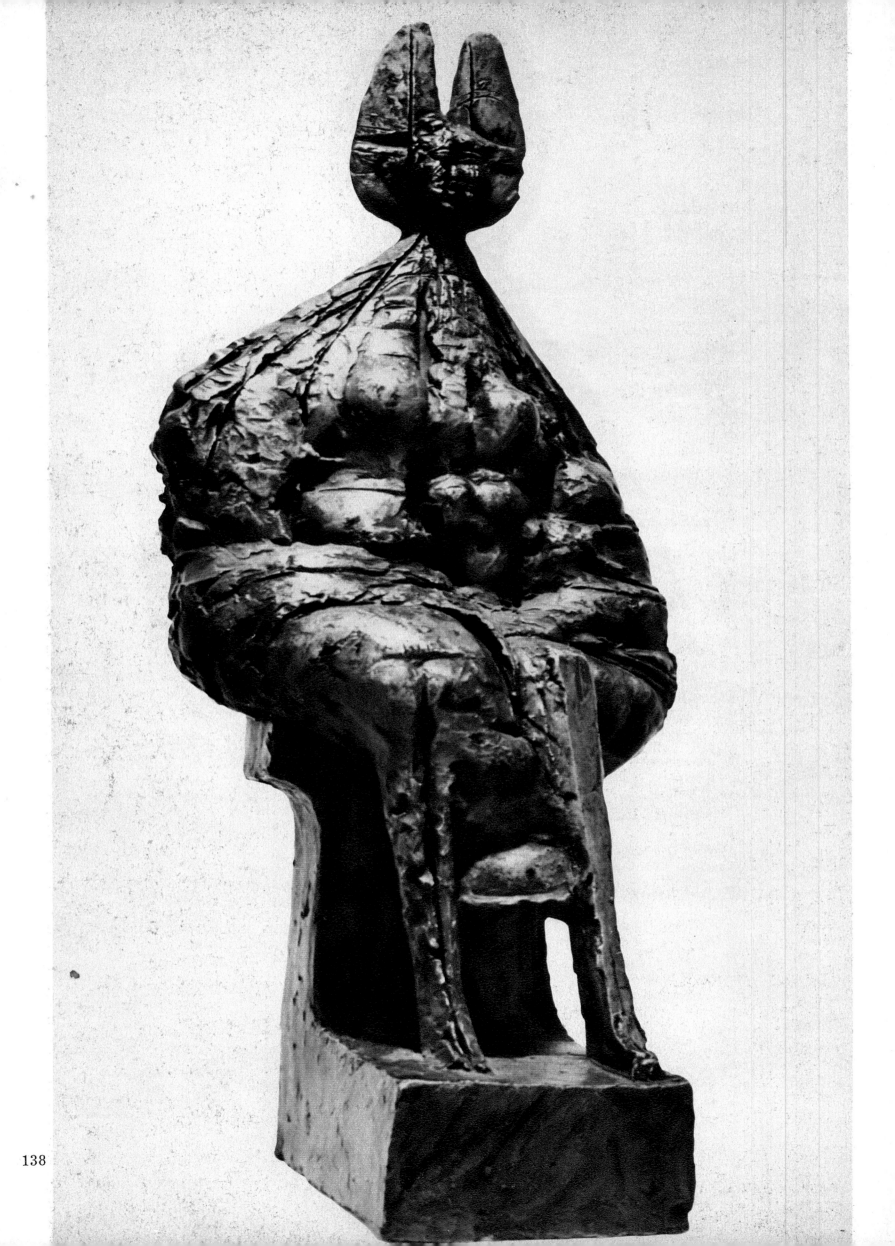

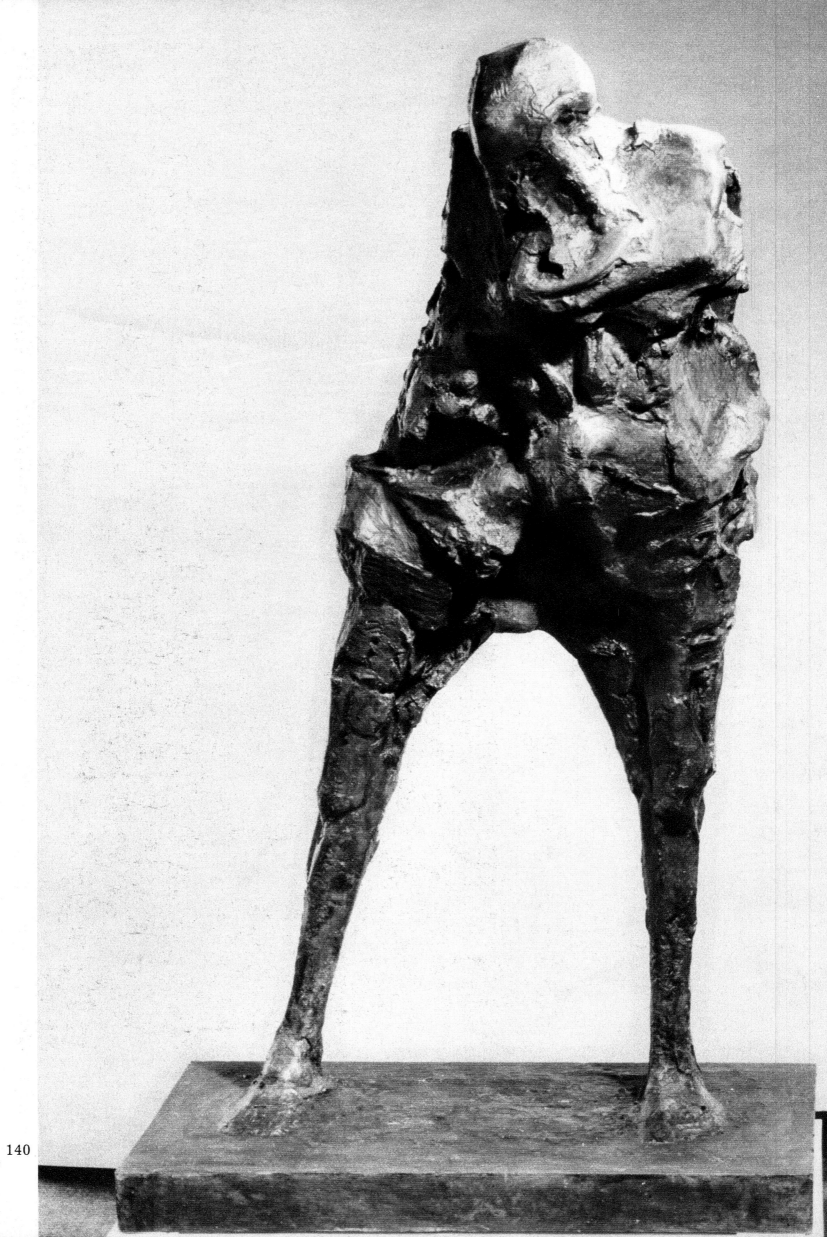

146

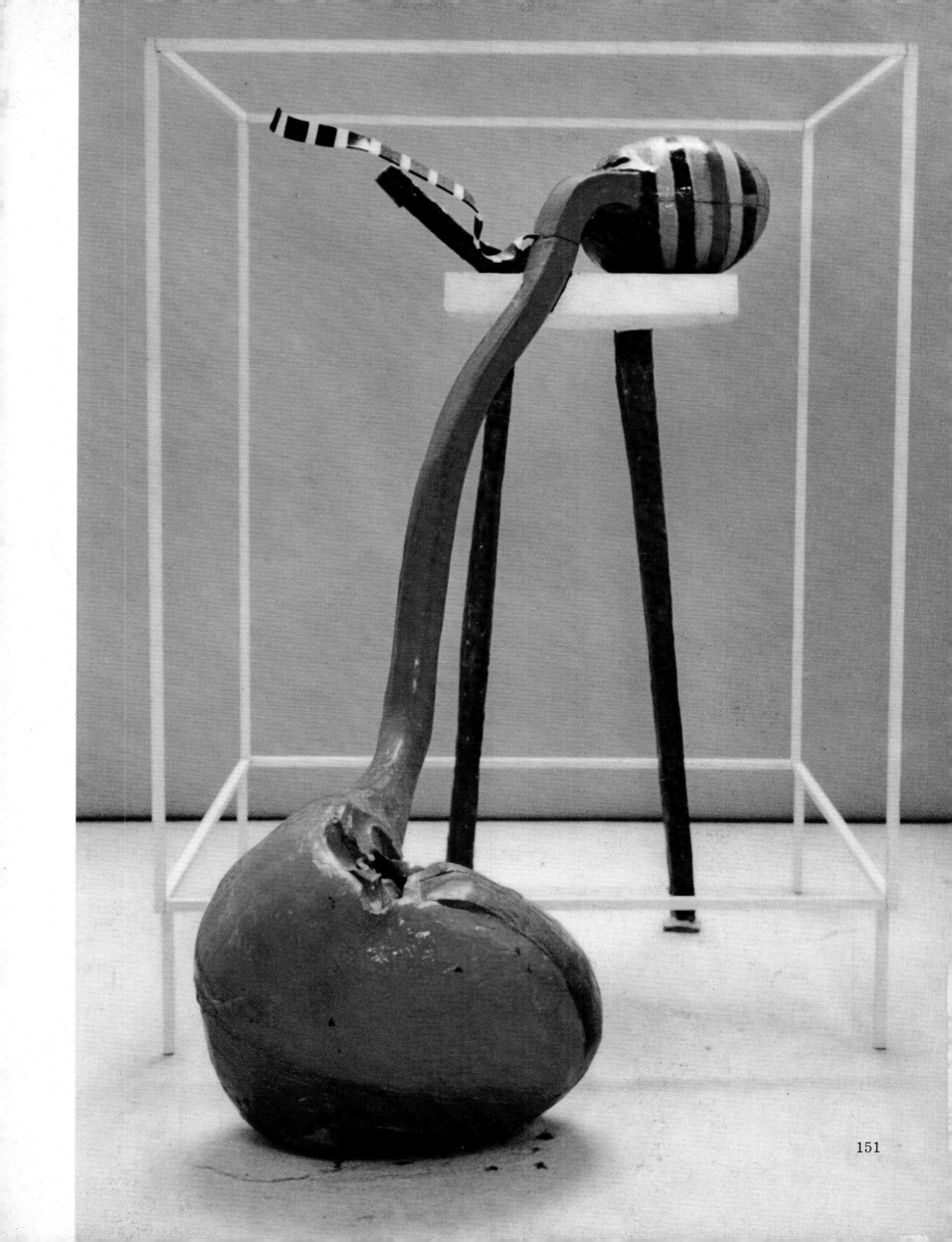

151

BIOGRAPHICAL NOTES

ADAMS, ROBERT. Born in 1917 in Northampton and trained at the Northampton School of Art. 1947, first one-man show: Gimpel Fils Gallery, London, then Galerie Jeanne Bucher, Paris. 1949-60, lecturer at the Central School of Arts and Crafts, London. 1952, represented at the Venice Biennale; 1957, at the São Paulo Biennal; 1962, one-man exhibition, British Pavilion, Venice Biennale.

Commissions include: 1951, Stone sculpture, King's Heath School, Northampton; 1959, Reinforced concrete wall relief for Stadtstheater, Gelsenkirchen, Germany; 1961, *Sunburst,* Basrelief Mural, P. and O. liner *Canberra.*

Works in following collections: Tate Gallery, London; Museum of Modern Art, New York; Albright-Knox Art Gallery, Buffalo; Museo de Bellas Artes, Caracas; Museum of Modern Art, São Paulo.

Bibliography: Recent British Sculpture, British Council Exhibition for Canada, New Zealand and Australia 1961-63 (Catalogue introduction by David Thompson); J.P. Hodin, 'Artist and Architect', recent monumental works produced in England, *Quadrum,* X, pp. 22-23, 1961; *Exhibition of Open Air Sculpture,* Battersea Park, London, 1963 (Catalogue).

ARMITAGE, KENNETH. Born 1916 in Leeds. 1934-37, studied at Leeds College of Art and 1937-39 at the Slade School, London. Served in the Army during the war. 1945-56, head of the sculpture department at the Bath Academy of Art. 1952, first one-man show: Gimpel Fils Gallery, London, and represented at the Venice Biennale. 1953-55, awarded the Gregory Fellowship in Sculpture at Leeds University. 1957, represented at the São Paulo Biennal. 1958, won the David E. Bright Foundation Award at the Venice Biennale.

Commissions include: 1957-58, *Triarchy,* new Berlin Opera House; 1960-63, *Mouton Sun.* Château Mouton Rothschild, near Bordeaux.

Works in following museums: Tate Gallery and Victoria and Albert Museum, London; Museum of Modern Art, New York; Albright-Knox Art Gallery, Buffalo; Musée National d'Art Moderne, Paris; Musées Royaux des Beaux-Arts, Brussels; Museo de Bellas Artes, Caracas; Rijksmuseum Kröller-Müller, Otterlo.

Bibliography: Alan Bowness, *Kenneth Armitage,* Whitechapel Gallery Exhibition, London, 1959 (Catalogue); Roland Penrose, *Kenneth Armitage,* Switzerland, 1960; Norbert Lynton, *Kenneth Armitage,* London, 1962 (contains a complete bibliography and list of exhibitions).

BROWN, RALPH. Born 1928 in Leeds. Studied 1948-51 Leeds College of Art, 1951-52 Hammersmith School of Art, 1952-56 Royal College of Art, London. 1954, spent six months in Paris and in 1955 visited Greece. 1956, in Italy. 1958, became lecturer at the Royal College of Art, London. 1961, first one-man show: Leicester Galleries, London.

Commissions include: Sculpture for Brussels World Fair, 1958; Market Place Fountain, Hatfield New Town.

Works in following museums: Tate Gallery, London; Rijksmuseum Kröller-Müller, Otterlo; National Museum of Wales, Cardiff.

Bibliography: Bryan Robertson, 'Ralph Brown, Sculptor', *Motif* 8, London, Winter 1961, p. 50.

BUTLER, REG. Born 1915 in Buntingford, Hertfordshire. Trained as architect. 1949, first one-man show: Hanover Gallery, London. In 1953, won the Grand Prize in the International Sculpture Competition for a Monument to the Unknown Political Prisoner. 1952 and 1954 exhibited at the Venice Biennale and in 1957 at the São Paulo Biennal.

Commissions include: 1951, *Birdcage,* Festival of Britain; 1952, *The Oracle,* Hatfield Technical College.

Works in following museums: Tate Gallery, London; Museum of Modern Art, New York; Baltimore Museum; Gemeente Museum, The Hague; Albright-Knox Art Gallery, Buffalo; Museum of Fine Arts, Boston; Brooklyn Museum.

Bibliography: Robert Melville, 'In connection with the sculpture of Reg Butler' *Motif* 6, London, Spring 1961.

CARO, ANTHONY. Born 1924 in London. During World War II served in the Fleet Air Arm of the Royal Navy and then took a degree in engineering at Cambridge. 1946, studied at the Regent Street Polytechnic. 1947-52, studied at the Royal Academy Art School, London. 1951-53, assistant to Henry Moore. Since 1953, has taught sculpture at St Martin's School of Art, London. 1956, first one-man show at the Galleria del Naviglio, Milan. 1959, exhibited at the 1st International Biennale des Jeunes, Paris, where he was awarded a six months grant to study in France. 1963, one-man exhibition, Whitechapel Art Gallery, London. Chosen for the British Section at the 32nd Venice Biennale, 1966.

Works in following museums: Tate Gallery and Victoria and Albert Museum, London.

Bibliography: Exhibition of Open Air Sculpture, Battersea Park, London, 1963 (Catalogue). One-man show, Whitechapel Art Gallery, London, 1963 (Catalogue).

CHADWICK, LYNN. Born 1914 in London. In 1933 graduated in architecture and practised as architect until 1939. During the war 1941-44 became a pilot in the Fleet Air Arm. In 1945 made his first experimental mobiles in collaboration with the architect Rodney Thomas. In 1946 produced his first independent works: textile and architectural designs for exhibitions. 1950, first one-man show: Gimpel Fils Gallery, London. In 1952 his 'balanced sculptures' were exhibited at the Venice Biennale; in 1956 he was awarded the International Sculture Prize at the 28th Venice Biennale. Chadwick has visited New York, Toronto, Paris, and Athens. 1961, represented in British Section at São Paulo Biennal. Since 1958 has lived at Lypiatt Park, Stroud, Gloucestershire.

Works in following museums: Tate Gallery, London; Musée National d'Art Moderne, Paris; Musée Royaux des Beaux-Arts, Brussels; Boymans-van Beuningen Museum, Rotterdam; Rijksmuseum Kröller-Müller, Otterlo; Museum of Modern Art, New York; National Gallery of Canada, Ottawa.

Bibliography: J.P. Hodin, *Lynn Chadwick,* London, 1961 (contains a complete bibliography and list of exhibitions); Herbert Read, *Lynn Chadwick,* Switzerland, 1958-60; Robert Melville, *Quadrum,* II, 1956, pp. 97-108; *L'Œil,* Paris, 1957, p. 226; Robert Melville, Catalogue Notes, British Pavilion, Venice, 1956 and Catalogue Introduction Pavilion des Beaux-Arts, Brussels, 1957; Alan Bowness, *Lynn Chadwick,* London, 1962.

CLARKE, GEOFFREY. Born 1924 in Derbyshire. Studied at the Lancaster School of Art. 1942-47, served in the Royal Air Force. 1948-52, studied at the Royal College of Art, London. 1952, first one-man show: Gimpel Fils Gallery, London. 1952, exhibited sculpture and 1960 prints at Venice Biennale.

Commissions include: 1952, *Wall Sculpture,* Time/Life Building, Bond Street, London; 1959, *Mosaic,* Physics Block, Liverpool University; 1959, *Relief,* Castrol Offices, Marylebone Road, London; 1953-62, *Flying Cross, High Altar Cross, Three Nave Windows,* and other works, Coventry Cathedral.

Works in following collections: The Arts Council of Great Britain, the British Council and Victoria and Albert Museum, London; Museum of Modern Art, New York.

Bibliography: Exhibition of Open Air Sculpture, Battersea Park, London, 1963 (Catalogue); *Geoffrey Clarke, recent sculptures,* Redfern Gallery, London, 1965 (Catalogue).

DALWOOD, HUBERT. Born 1924 in Bristol. 1939-45, worked as an apprentice designer at the British Aeroplane Company. 1946-49, studied under Kenneth Armitage at the Bath Academy of Art. 1951, won Italian Government Scholarship and studied in Italy. 1954, first one-man exhibition: Gimpel Fils Gallery, London. 1955-58, held the Gregory Fellowship in Sculpture at Leeds University. 1956-64, taught at Leeds College of Art and the Royal College of Art, London. 1962, one-man exhibition, British Pavilion, Venice Biennale. 1964, appointed Visiting Professor at the University of Illinois, Urbana.

Commissions include: 1959, large outdoor sculpture for Physics Block, Liverpool University; 1959, Screen, Ionian Bank, London.

Works in following museums: Tate Gallery and Victoria and Albert Museum, London; Museum of Modern Art, New York; Solomon R. Guggenheim Museum, New York; Albright-Knox Art Gallery, Buffalo.

Bibliography: Hubert Dalwood, Gimpel Fils Gallery, London, September 1964 (Catalogue); Norbert Lynton, 'Hubert Dalwood' *Quadrum,* VIII, pp. 146-47.

EPSTEIN, SIR JACOB. Born 1880 in New York and died 1959 in London. Trained as a sculptor with George Grey Barnard (1863-1938) in New York. He produced illustrations for *The Spirit of the Ghetto* by Hutchins Hapgood, published 1902. 1901, worked in a bronze foundry. 1902, went to Paris where he studied at the Ecole des Beaux-Arts and the Académie Julien. Came to England in 1905 and became British citizen in 1907. Made contact with Augustus John, Ambrose McEvoy, Muirhead Bone and Francis Dodd. In 1907 was commissioned to carve eighteen statues for the British Medical Association building in the Strand, London. These statues caused a storm of controversy and were destroyed by the Rhodesian Government in 1937. He remained in Paris for six months and met Picasso, Modigliani, Brancusi and Paul Guillaume. Began to form his large collection of Cycladic, African, Oceanic and Egyptian sculpture. 1916-18, in the armed forces. First one-man show: Leicester Galleries, London, 1917. 1927, travelled to U.S.A. returning to London in 1928 to live at 18, Hyde Park Gate.

Commissions include: 1909, *Tomb of Oscar Wilde* (erected 1912), cemetery of Père-Lachaise, Paris; 1925, *Rima,* Hyde Park, London; 1929, carvings for London Transport building; 1949, many commissions including *Youth Advancing* (Festival of Britain); 1950, *Madonna and Child,* Cavendish Square, London; 1951, *Social Consciousness,* Fairmount Park Association, Philadelphia; 1954, *Liverpool Resurgent,* Lewis's Ltd., Liverpool; 1955, *Christ in Majesty,* Llandaff Cathedral; 1956-57, *War Memorial,* Trades Union Congress Building, London; 1958, *St Michael and the Devil,* Coventry Cathedral; 1959, Bowater House Group, London.

Works in following collections: Tate Gallery, London and many other public and private collections in Great Britain.

Bibliography: Epstein, *The Sculptor Speaks,* London, 1931; Epstein, *Let There Be Sculpture,* London, 1940; *Epstein, an Autobiography,* London, 1963 (reprint with an Introduction by Richard Buckle); Richard Buckle, *Jacob Epstein, Sculptor,* London, 1963.

FRINK, ELIZABETH. Born 1930 at Thurlow, Suffolk. 1947-49, studied at the Guildford School of Art and from 1949-53 at the Chelsea School of Art. 1959, first one-man show: Waddington Galleries, London.

Commissions include: 1951, *Wild Boar,* Harlow New Town and large bronze *Blind Man and Dog* for Bethnal Green Housing Scheme, London; 1960, Copper relief, façade Carlton Tower Hotel, London.

Works in following museums: Tate Gallery, London; National Gallery of Victoria, Melbourne.

Bibliography: J.P. Hodin, *Quadrum,* X, pp. 148-149.

FULLARD, GEORGE. Born 1924 in Sheffield. 1939-42, studied at the Sheffield College of Art. 1942-44, military service in World War II. 1945-48, studied at Royal College of Art, London. 1964, first one-man show: New London Gallery, London. Now teaches at Chelsea School of Art, London.

Works in following collections: Arts Council of Great Britain; Lannan Foundation, Chicago; National Gallery of South Australia, Adelaide.

Bibliography: Jasia Reichardt, 'George Fullard and the Menacing Baby Saint', *Metro* 9, 1965.

GAUDIER-BRZESKA, HENRI. Born 1891 in St-Jean-de-Braye, France and spent his youth in Orléans. 1908, won scholarship to London and Bristol and in 1909 was sent by Bristol University to study art in Germany. Returning to Paris in 1910 he met Sophie Brzeska and at this point decided to become a sculptor. 1911, left Paris for London with Sophie, changing his name to Gaudier-Brzeska. 1911-14, in London where he became the friend of many writers and artists including Middleton Murry, Ezra Pound (his first biographer), Horace Brodsky, Katherine Mansfield and Roger Fry. Joined the French Army in 1914 and was killed in action in June 1914 at Neuville-St-Vaast. 1918, first one-man show: Leicester Galleries, London.

Works in following museums: Musée National d'Art Moderne, Paris; Tate Gallery, London.

Bibliography: Catalogue prefaces: 1918, Ezra Pound (Leicester Galleries); 1956, René Varin and Jacqueline Auzar-Pruvost (Orléans, Musée des Beaux-Arts); 1956, Philip James and J. Wood Palmer (Arts Council of Great Britain); 1962, Leicester Galleries, London (Exhibition catalogue with biographical note). Ezra Pound, *Gaudier-Brzeska: A Memoir*, London, 1916; H.S. Ede, *A life of Gaudier-Brzeska*, London, 1930, also *Savage Messiah*, London, 1931; Horace Brodsky, *Henri Gaudier-Brzeska*, London, 1933, also *Gaudier-Brzeska, Drawings*, London, 1946; *Quadrum*, III, p. 180. Illustration of a sculpture entitled 'Stags' from The Art Institute of Chicago (with note by J.P. Hodin); *Gaudier-Brzeska; Drawings and Sculpture* (with an introduction by Mervyn Levy), London, 1965.

HEPWORTH, DAME BARBARA. Born 1903 in Wakefield, Yorkshire. 1920 studied at Leeds School of Art and from 1921 to 1924 at the Royal College of Art in London. Between 1924 and 1925 studied the 'taille directe' technique of carving in marble under the sculptor Ardini. 1927, first exhibition at the London Studio, St John's Wood, together with her first husband John Skeaping. 1927-30, living in Hampstead. 1937, married Ben Nicholson (divorced 1951). 1932, in Paris where she met Arp, Brancusi, Picasso, Calder, Miró and Braque. 1933-34, a member of the group 'Unit One' formed in London; came into contact with Mondrian, Gabo, Moholy-Nagy. Since 1939 has lived at St Ives, Cornwall. 1950, a retrospective exhibition of her sculpture held at the 25th Venice Biennale. 1954, visited Greece. 1959, won Grand Prix at the 5th Biennal, São Paulo. 1954 and 1962, further retrospective exhibitions held at the Whitechapel Gallery, London. 1964-66, retrospective exhibition of sculptures and drawings has toured Europe; Copenhagen, Stockholm, Helsinki, Oslo, Otterlo (Holland), Zurich, Turin, Karlsruhe and Essen.

Commissions include: Theme in Electronics, Mullard House, London; *Winged Figure*, John Lewis Building, London; *Monolith*, Kenwood House, Hampstead; *Contrapuntal Forms*, Harlow New Town; *Vertical Forms*, Hatfield Technical College; *Single Form*, Dag Hammarskjöld Memorial, United Nations Building, New York.

Works in following museums: Tate Gallery, London; Museum of Modern Art, New York; Albright-Knox Art Gallery, Buffalo; Walker Art Center, Minneapolis; National Gallery of Canada, Ottawa; Rijksmuseum Kröller-Müller, Otterlo.

Bibliography: William Gibson, *Barbara Hepworth*, London, 1946; Herbert Read, *Barbara Hepworth, Carvings and Drawings*, London, 1952 (with an autobiographical note); J.P. Hodin, 'Artist and Architect', *Quadrum*, X, pp. 24-26; J.P. Hodin, *Barbara Hepworth, Her Life and Work*, Neuchâtel and London 1961 (with full information, bibliography and complete catalogue by Alan Bowness); A.M. Hammacher, *Barbara Hepworth*, Amsterdam and London, 1958.

HOSKIN, JOHN. Born 1921 in Cheltenham, Gloucestershire. Trained as architectural draughtsman. 1942-47, army service, started painting and designing. 1950, worked as truck-driver while studying abstract art. 1950, first one-man show: Matthiesen Gallery, London. 1957, instructor at the Bath Academy of Art, Corsham Court. Lives in Swindon, Wiltshire.

Works in following museums: Tate Gallery and Victoria and Albert Museum, London; Birmingham City Museum and Art Gallery; National Gallery of South Australia, Adelaide. *Works in following churches:* St Stephen's, Southmead, Bristol (1959); Nuffield College Chapel, Oxford (1961).

Bibliography: J.P. Hodin, *Quadrum*, XI, pp. 150-151.

KING, PHILLIP. Born 1934 in Tunis. 1954-57, read Modern Languages at Cambridge University. 1957, first one-man show: Heffers Gallery, Cambridge. 1957-58, studied at St Martin's School of Art, London. 1958-59, assistant to Henry Moore. 1950, awarded Boise Scholarship to Greece for three months. 1961, included in a group show of British sculpture in Madrid. 1963, chosen for the British Section of the 3rd Biennale des Jeunes, Paris; 1964, first one-man show in London at the Rowan Gallery. Now teaches at St Martin's School of Art, London.

Works in following collections: Arts Council of Great Britain; the Calouste Gulbenkian Foundation; and the Tate Gallery, London.

Bibliography: The New Generation: 1965, Whitechapel Gallery, London, March-April, 1965 (Catalogue). Jasia Reichardt, 'Sculpture in Colour', *Quadrum* 18, pp. 71-78, 1965.

MARTIN, KENNETH. Born 1905 in Sheffield. Studied Sheffield School of Art. 1929-32, Royal College of Art, London. Started as landscape painter. 1951, made his first mobile constructions basing his approach to sculpture on his study of mathematics and science. Now lives in Hampstead.

Works in following collections: Victoria and Albert Museum, London, Arts Council of Great Britain.

Bibliography: Lawrence Alloway, *Nine Abstract Artists,* London, 1954; *The World of Abstract Art,* edited by 'The American Abstract Artists', New York, 1957; Andrew Forge 'Notes on the Mobiles of Kenneth Martin', *Quadrum,* III, pp. 93-98, 1957; J.P. Hodin, 'Une fontaine en acier inoxydable de Kenneth Martin', *Quadrum,* XII, p. 169, 1961; Kenneth Martin, 'Kinetics', *Architectural Design,* December, 1963.

MEADOWS, BERNARD. Born 1915 in Norwich. Studied at the Norwich School of Art and then at the Chelsea School of Art and the Royal College, London. 1936-40, assistant to Henry Moore. He has taught sculpture at the Chelsea School of Art and at the Bath Academy of Art, Corsham. Since 1960 he has been Professor of Sculpture at the Royal College of Art, London. 1957, first one-man show: Gimpel Fils Gallery, London. Represented at the Venice Biennale in 1952, also at the São Paulo Biennal, 1957; one-man exhibition, British Pavilion, Venice Biennale, 1964.

Works in following museums: Tate Gallery, and Victoria and Albert Museum, London; Museum of Modern Art, New York; Solomon R. Guggenheim Museum, New York; Yale Art Gallery; San Francisco Museum of Art; Museo de Bellas Artes, Caracas.

Bibliography: J.P. Hodin, *Quadrum,* VI, p. 158, 1959.

MOORE, HENRY. Born 1898 in Castleford, Yorkshire. Until 1916 taught in Castleford. 1917, joined the army. Was gassed in the battle of Cambrai. 1919, on leaving the army attended the Leeds School of Art. 1921, became student at the Royal College of Art, London and travelled in Italy and France on a scholarship. Remained as a teacher at the Royal College until 1931. 1928, first one-man show: Warren Gallery, London, and received his first commission for reliefs on the London Transport Building in St James's. 1933, became a member of the 'Unit One' group. Between 1931 and 1939 taught at the Chelsea School of Art. 1940-42, became an official War Artist. 1948, won the International Prize at the 24th Venice Biennale. 1953, won the International Prize at the 2nd São Paulo Biennal.

Commissions include: 1943-44, *Madonna and Child,* St Matthew's Church, Northampton; 1943-46, *Memorial Figure,* Dartington Hall, Devon; 1947-48, *Madonna and Child,* St Peter's Church, Claydon, Suffolk; 1949, *Family Group,* Barclay School, Stevenage; 1957-58, *Reclining Figure,* Unesco Headquarters, Paris; 1963-65, *Reclining Figure,* Lincoln Center, New York.

Works in following collections: Tate Gallery, London; Musée National d'Art Moderne, Paris; Museum of Modern Art, New York; National Gallery of Canada, Ottawa; National Gallery of Victoria, Melbourne; Museo de Arte Moderna, Rio de Janeiro; Rijksmuseum Kröller-Müller, Otterlo, and many other public and private collections.

Selected Bibliography: Arts Council of Great Britain, *Sculpture and Drawings by Henry Moore,* Tate Gallery, London, 1951 (Catalogue prepared by A.D.B. Sylvester on the occasion of the Festival of Britain); Herbert Read, *Henry Moore, Sculpture and Drawings,* Vol. I (1921-1948) 4th edition, edited by David Sylvester; Vol. II (since 1948); Vol. III (1955-64), London 1957, 1955, 1965; J.P. Hodin, *Henry Moore,* London, 1958; Herbert Read, *Henry Moore, A study of his Life and Work,* London, 1965.

MORLAND, FRANCIS. Born 1934 in Norfolk. 1954-57, studied sculpture at the Slade School of Fine Arts, London. 1962, first one-man show; New Vision Centre Gallery, London. 1963, his work included in the 3rd Paris Biennale des Jeunes. Since 1964 has taught at St Martin's School of Art, London.

Works in following collections: Arts Council of Great Britain; Leeds University.

MOSS, MARLOW. Born 1890 in Richmond, Surrey. Died 1958, Penzance, Cornwall. Until 1919, at the St John's Wood School of Art, The Slade School and the School of Art, Penzance, Cornwall. 1927, first contact with the work of Mondrian in Paris. 1928, studied under Léger and Ozenfant. First exhibited in Paris. 1929, produced her first abstract compositions. Became a member of 'Les Surindépendants'. From 1929 until 1938 regular meetings with Mondrian. 1940, the entire output of her work up to that year was destroyed in her studio at Gauciel (France). 1940, returned to Cornwall. 1953, first one-man show: Hanover Gallery, London. 1962, Memorial Exhibition at the Stedelijk Museum, Amsterdam.

Bibliography: Hanover Gallery Exhibition 1958 (Catalogue introduction by Michel Seuphor); Memorial Exhibition, Stedelijk Museum, Amsterdam, 1962 (Catalogue No. 301, introduction by A.M. Nijhoff).

PAOLOZZI, EDUARDO. Born 1924 in Edinburgh of Italian parents. 1943, attended the College of Art, Edinburgh. 1944-47, Slade School of Fine Arts, London. 1947, first one-man show: Mayor Gallery, London. 1947-50, worked in Paris where he made contact with Léger, Braque, Brancusi, Giacometti and the surrealist milieu of Tzara and Leiris. 1951, made a fountain for the South Bank Exhibition, London, during the Festival of Britain. 1952, represented at the Venice Biennale. 1949-55, taught textile-design at the Central School of Arts and Crafts, London. 1949-58, taught sculpture at St Martin's School of Art, London. Awarded Bright Foundation Award on one-man exhibition in British Pavilion, Venice Biennale, 1960.

Commissions include: (between 1950-54); Mural reliefs for the flats of Maxwell Fry and Jane Drew, London; reliefs and a ceiling, Institute of Contemporary Arts, London; wallpaper and textile-designs for Coles of Mortimer Street, David Whitehead and Sons Ltd., and Horrocks and Co., London; and a fountain for a park in Hamburg, 1953.

Works in following museums: Tate Gallery, London; Museum of Modern Art, New York; Solomon R. Guggenheim Museum, New York; Albright-Knox Art Gallery, Buffalo; Rijksmuseum Kröller-Müller, Otterlo.

Bibliography: J.P. Hodin, *Quadrum,* I, pp. 184-185, 1956; Robert Melville British Pavilion Exhibition, 30th Venice Biennale (Catalogue introduction).

PICHÉ, ROLAND. Born 1938 in London. 1956-60, studied at Hornsey College of Art. 1960-64, studied at the Royal College of Art, London. Since 1964 has taught at Maidstone School of Art, Kent. Lives in Essex. Represented Paris Biennale des Jeunes, 1965.

Works in following collections: Royal College of Art, London.

Bibliography: The New Generation: 1965, Whitechapel Gallery, London, March-April 1965 (Catalogue).

RICHMOND, OLIFFE. Born 1919 in Tasmania. Studied at East Sydney Technical College. 1948, enrolled at the Chelsea School of Art. Assistant to Henry Moore until 1950. Teacher at Chelsea School of Art and Hornsey College of Art. 1962, first one-man show: Molton Gallery, London.

Works in following collections: Arts Council of Great Britain, London; Rijksmuseum Kröller-Müller, Otterlo; L.C.C. William Penn School, Camberwell.

TURNBULL, WILLIAM. Born 1922 in Dundee. 1947-48, studied at the Slade School of Fine Arts. 1948-50, studied in Paris. 1949, produced his first mobile-stabile. 1950, first one-man show: Hanover Gallery, London. Since 1951, has acted as visiting lecturer at the Central School of Arts and Crafts, London. 1952, represented Venice Biennale, and 1957 at the São Paulo Biennal. Also exhibits painting regularly.

Works in following museums: Tate Gallery, London; Albright-Knox Art Gallery, Buffalo.

Bibliography: 'William Turnbull, Painter Sculptor' *Upper Case* 4, (edited by Theo Gosby with Notes by Turnbull), London, 1960; Lawrence Alloway, Molton Gallery Exhibition, London; 1960 (Catalogue introduction).

UNDERWOOD, LEON. Born 1890 in London. Studied at the Royal College of Art and the Slade. 1923, first one-man show in London. Introduced elements of primitive and exotic sculpture into European sculpture. 1928, studied Mayan and Aztec sculpture. Has travelled extensively in Mexico, Africa, Iceland, Canada and the U.S. 1945, studied Negro art in South Africa.

Commissions include: 1960, *Ideas,* Hilgrove Housing Estate, Finchley Road, London.

Works in following museums: Tate Gallery, British Museum and Victoria and Albert Museum, London.

Bibliography: J.P. Hodin, 'Leon Underwood' *Quadrum,* X, pp. 20-22. Underwood's own writings include: *Figures in Wood of West Africa,* London, 1947; *Masks of West Africa,* London, 1948; *Bronzes of West Africa,* London, 1949.

WITKIN, ISAAC. Born 1936 in Johannesburg. Worked as a sculptor's apprentice in South Africa. 1956, came to England. 1957-60, studied at St Martin's School of Art, London. 1961-64, assistant to Henry Moore. 1963, first one-man show: Rowan Gallery, London. 1963-65, taught at St Martin's School of Art, London. Represented Paris Biennale des Jeunes, 1965.

Works in following collections: Arts Council of Great Britain and Gulbenkian Foundation, London.

Bibliography: The New Generation: 1965, Whitechapel Gallery, London, March-April 1965 (Catalogue). Jasia Reichardt, 'Sculpture in Colour', *Quadrum* 18, pp. 71-78, 1965.

LIST OF ILLUSTRATIONS

ACKNOWLEDGEMENTS

I would like to thank all the artists, the Directors of galleries and museums, and the photographers who have provided information and illustrations of the works I selected to be reproduced.

Above all my gratitude goes to the Fine Art Department of the British Council, directed by Mrs Lilian Somerville, whose staff-members, especially Miss Margaret McLeod, were very helpful.

Among the artists, I want to thank particularly Henry Moore who provided a great number of his own photographs, as did Lynn Chadwick. Dame Barbara Hepworth personally assisted the photographer Mr. John Webb with his work in and outside her studio.

The supervision of the translation of the text and the biographical notes was in the hands of Miss Patricia Lowman. I am particularly indebted to her for her generous assistance.

A.M. HAMMACHER